"An innovative integration of science and soul —this practical guide reclaims aging as a sacred, empowered journey."
—Dr. Pearl E. Gregor, PhD, Education & Philosophy

LIVING AND AGING WELL

A Practical and Holistic Guide for Older Adults, Families and Helping Professionals

KATHLEEN CESARIN, LPN
WELLNESS COACH, HEALTHCARE NAVIGATOR
& EDUCATOR, REIKI MASTER-TEACHER

What the Experts Are Saying

"*Living & Aging Well* is the most relevant book I've ever read for this stage of life. As a retired health & safety coordinator and school board trustee, I found it to be exceptionally professional, deeply moving, and full of wisdom. It evoked powerful reflection and offered practical, timely guidance—especially on topics like downsizing and letting go—that truly resonated. This remarkable book provides essential information and resources to help make thoughtful decisions before it's too late. Every older adult, their family members, and professionals working with seniors should run out and get a copy today."

— Cecil Mackesey,
Retired Health & Safety Coordinator and School Board Trustee

"Kathleen's book is a comprehensive and highly practical guide that I wholeheartedly recommend—especially for those supporting older adults through life transitions. As a veteran and long-time community service leader, I truly appreciated the book's accessible layout, insightful innovations in living options and assistive technologies, and the real-life tools for downsizing and home selling. The Living & Aging Well Readiness Assessment is an excellent starting point for self-evaluation, and the Grab & Go Vital Records Organizer is a standout resource—easy to complete and invaluable in both daily life and times of crisis. This book is a must-have for older adults and those who care for them."

— Montgomery Johnson,
CD, Veteran, Past President & Community Services Leader,
Rotary Club of Morinville Sturgeon; Board Member,
Morinville Sturgeon Men's Shed Club

"Kathleen's immense heart and experience as a nurse and wellness practitioner shine through in *Living and Aging Well*, a comprehensive guide to assist older adults, family members, and caregivers.

This guide is easy to read and provides opportunities to discuss, learn, and apply information about topics to assist people in aging in a healthy manner and to guide people to make important, balanced decisions.

As a licensed nurse, for nearly twenty years, working in acute care medicine, I encounter many concerns from older adults (for example, financial concerns about housing, moving to long-term care, etc.). The information in this guide is very relevant to the needs of our aging population, and I highly recommend it as tool for other helping professionals."

— *Stephanie Wilson, Registered Nurse, BN*

"In this guide, Kathleen offers practical and helpful ways you can listen to older adults in your family or community and discuss their wants and needs as they age. She offers guidelines that will assist you in discovering the most useful questions as older adults and seniors grapple with the challenges of decisions about where they want to live, current and future financial needs, health and personal needs. This guide is designed to help you personally and professionally work with both intention and respect in collaboration with older adults and seniors to meet both current and future goals and aspirations."

— *Dr. Pearl Gregor, PhD, Author, Dream Coach*

"Finally, someone has had the vision to create a far-reaching, no-nonsense, down-to-earth guide that covers every area imaginable in planning for the later years of life. With nearly thirty years in this field, I've seen many resources—but nothing like this. Kathleen has pulled together a truly comprehensive, easy-to-follow format that speaks to the heart and the practical side of aging.

Living & Aging Well is the kind of wide-ranging tool that belongs in the hands of hospitals, universities, retirement communities, estate planners, lawyers, caregivers, financial advisors, and anyone supporting older adults.

It's professionally written, thoughtfully organized, and generous in its scope—a journey of the heart that offers real guidance through every step of aging, retirement, and beyond. I encourage you to use this book for your clients, your family, and anyone else you care about. They'll benefit immensely."

— Derrick Cunningham,
Licensed Financial Advisor/Agent & Certified Branch Manager,
PFSL Investments Canada Ltd.

"I am so impressed with this resource. Kathleen has truly thought of everything that seniors and family members could need. I know this book will be in my library to help my clients."

— Steven Krahn, B.Ed., Retirement Living Consultant

My Intentions and A Letter of Thanks

Throughout my personal and professional journey—whether in healthcare, social work, or education—I've come to believe, deeply and unwaveringly, that **outcomes, relationships, and real connection are always more successful when we see and treat people as whole beings: mind, body, soul, and spirit.**

Even when our role does not require us to engage with all aspects of a person's wholeness, simply acknowledging their full humanity—seeing them through a holistic lens—naturally cultivates greater empathy, compassion, and wisdom. This perspective has guided me through every chapter of my career, whether working in an emergency room; operating my Accelerated Cast Clinic & Limb Preservation Centre to care for broken bones, feet, or wounds; supporting someone through a suicide crisis; giving foster children a place to call home; or offering one-on-one healing sessions, educational workshops, or retreats. In every encounter, I have always endeavored to see and support the whole person, in any way I can.

This book is more than a collection of information—it is a heartfelt offering. **I set out to create a universal, person-centered, and holistic resource that encourages meaningful, open, and progressive conversations about aging.**

Over the years, I have witnessed with concern how our healthcare and support systems often operate in silos—where plans and decisions are made *for* people instead of *with* them, where we treat one area while ignoring the whole that is suffering. This pattern not only disempowers individuals but disregards the depth of their lived experience.

I believe we can do better.

With this resource, my hope is to inspire a more respectful, collaborative, and compassionate approach to aging—one where older adults, their loved ones, and helping professionals engage in **genuine, balanced dialogue, with dignity, appreciation, and empathy at the core.**

I intentionally designed this book to be accessible, easy to read and apply, and simple to teach. It flows naturally, offering concise, practical tools that reduce common barriers to navigating aging-related decision-making. Whether you are an older adult seeking to age with intention, a family member navigating this journey alongside a loved one, or a healthcare or community professional providing support, this resource is meant **to empower you with clarity, confidence, and connection.**

I want to express my gratitude to the **Town of Morinville**—the community where I currently reside and where I chose to begin my "older adult" years at the age of fifty-one in 2023. The warmth, support, and spirit of this town have inspired and encouraged me. I am grateful to walk this path of aging well and intentionally create the future I desire—for myself, my family, my community, and all who read this resource.

***To my friends, family, and especially my three adult children**—Andrew, Bryant, and Michayla—and my husband, Tyler: your unwavering support, patience, and belief in my passions mean the world to me. You've embraced my ongoing journey of personal growth and my commitment to being the change I wish to see in the world, no matter how many projects, transformations, or versions of myself that has included. For that, I am deeply and endlessly grateful.*

It is my sincere hope that *Living & Aging Well* not only offers practical guidance but also sparks deeper compassion, connection, and understanding for all who embark on the journey of aging—together. **Thank you from my heart**.

Kathleen Cesarin

Welcome to Philosophia Within

Kathleen Cesarin, LPN

Kathleen Cesarin is the founder of *Philosophia Within* and a dedicated nurse, educator, and wellness practitioner with over twenty-five years of experience. Blending traditional healthcare expertise with alternative healing practices, she empowers individuals to embrace holistic wellness of the mind, body, soul, and spirit. Through her compassionate approach, Kathleen offers healthcare navigation, Reiki/biofield energy healing, and wellness coaching—helping others find balance, resilience, and clarity on their personal wellness journeys.

With a lifelong passion for teaching and learning and a deep commitment to making a positive impact, she strives to inspire meaningful connections and foster a loving, balanced approach to well-being.

Looking for an engaging speaker, workshop facilitator, or retreat leader?

Kathleen brings expertise, passion, and a holistic approach to wellness, offering transformative experiences for individuals and groups.

- ☀ **Book a Presentation or Workshop** – Host an interactive session on wellness, self-care, aging, or personal growth.
- ☀ **Plan a Retreat** – Bring deeper healing and renewal to your group with a customized retreat experience.
- ☀ **Access Wellness Services & Resources** – Explore coaching, healthcare navigation, Reiki, and holistic wellness support.
- ☀ **Discover Online Courses & Products** – Learn and grow at your own pace with curated courses and wellness tools.

Let's create a future of clarity, confidence, and care— together.

For more information, visit: **www.philosophiawithin.com**

Intellectual Property Notice and Thank you

Thank you for purchasing this material. This content is the intellectual property of Philosophia Within and is protected by copyright law. Unauthorized reproduction, distribution, or resale—whether in print or digital form—is strictly prohibited without written permission. Instead of copying or selling this material, I encourage you to share my work by directing others to my official offerings.

Together we can spread wisdom and information in a way that respects the integrity of this work. Thank you for honoring this request and being part of this community. Your support allows me to continue creating meaningful resources to help others thrive, grow, and find healing and balance.

If you found this information helpful, please:

- ☀ **Leave a review** - Your feedback makes a difference!
- ☀ **Follow and share on social media** - Help spread the wisdom.
- ☀ **Reach out** - Have suggestions or questions? Let's make it better!

Facebook: facebook.com/philosophiawithin
Instagram: @philosophiawithin
Shop & Explore More @ philosophiawithin.com

Your wellness journey starts within. Thank you for allowing me to be part of it!

Kathleen Cesarin, LPN

Philosophia
— WITHIN —

Special Thanks!
To those who shared their stories, helped edit and reviewed this material to add their wisdom and insights.

I am deeply appreciative and grateful.

ISBN: 979-8-89989-031-4 (eBook)
ISBN: 979-8-89989-032-1 (Paperback)
ISBN: 979-8-89989-033-8 (Hardcover)

Who Benefits from This Guide?

 ## Individuals/ Families

Older adults and their loved ones can use this guide to navigate decisions about living and aging well, downsizing, or transitioning to a new living arrangement. It includes helpful tools, checklists, and discussion points to guide informed choices in manageable, easy-to-understand sections—to be well prepared for a health crisis or emergency.

 ## Community Workshops/ Support Groups

Facilitators can use the planner as a foundation for group discussions, workshops, or educational sessions, providing participants with valuable insights and practical tools. Each section is thoughtfully designed to stand alone for ease of reference and distribution to participants.

 ## Helping Professionals/ Postsecondary Programs

Social workers, healthcare providers, college/university curriculum developers, retirement consultants, public libraries, and financial planners can incorporate this planner into their work with clients, offering structured guidance and easy-to-separate resources.

 ## Senior Centers/Retirement Facilities

This guide can serve as a resource for older adult and senior programs, offering guidance to those exploring their options for future living arrangements. Staff can use this planner to assist potential residents and their families in making informed, confident decisions.

Table of Contents

Let's Discuss

Let's define and imagine what "living and aging well" in mind, body, soul, and spirit can look like. Together.

"I have the power to shape a future filled with joy, purpose, and connection. Each choice I make today brings me closer to the life I envision."
— **My Soul**

Who *Is* an Older Adult Anyway?

When I first started working part-time in adult and senior programming, I asked what I thought was a simple, logical question: "Who *is* an older adult?" And let me tell you, the reactions were priceless. Some chuckled. Some dodged the question entirely. Others looked at me like I had just accused them of being ancient relics from a forgotten past. For the record, two years ago, I was fifty when I asked that question. Was I—gasp—an older adult? I sure didn't feel like it! But that's the thing, isn't it? The definition of *older adult* is murky, subjective, and constantly evolving.

Back in the day—let's say thirty years ago—the terms *elderly, senior, aged,* and *past your prime* were casually thrown around. These words conjured up images of white-haired, cardigan-clad folks in rocking chairs or playing bridge. The age? Usually pegged somewhere north of sixty-five. But let's face it, that stereotype has aged poorly (pun intended). These days, people over sixty- five might be training for marathons, running businesses, or posting TikTok's about their adventures in Portugal.

In recent years, the language has shifted again—now we hear terms like *active ager, vintage adult, young-at-heart,* or simply *55-plus community,* as if aging were a loyalty program. In this book, I use words such as *senior, elder,* and *older adult* interchangeably for inclusivity. Yet language continues to evolve, and with it a sensitivity that challenges old labels—making it tricky to clearly label or define a target audience. Perhaps the most inclusive option is to simply use the word *adult* - maybe by the next edition of this book, we'll all be ready for that.

As a nurse and wellness advocate with decades of experience, I've worked with people of all ages and backgrounds. But nothing prepared me for the existential amusement of being hired

to serve older adults and then wondering if I was one of them. Being an A-type personality, I did what any logic-loving human would do: the math. If adulthood starts at eighteen, and most services define *senior* as sixty-five, then the halfway mark is forty-five. So, mathematically speaking, anyone over forty-five is technically an *older adult*. Cue internal crisis and philosophical musings.

But here's where it got interesting: I started asking around. Colleagues who were five years younger or older than I was didn't want to be lumped into the *older adult* category. Some were amused. Others were offended. And still, no one had a clear answer. Meanwhile, marketing materials for older adult programs I researched featured mostly white-haired, Caucasian women, clearly over seventy-five. That didn't reflect the full spectrum of those who could benefit from these programs—not by a long shot.

So, I took a step back. I considered the shifting lifestyles of my own Gen-X cohort compared to my parents' *boomer* generation, and my kids—millennial and Gen Z. We're living longer, working differently, learning constantly, and breaking stereotypes daily. Technology, mobility, values, and social expectations are transforming what it means to be an *older adult*. And that transformation needs to be reflected in how we define and serve this group.

Ultimately, I chose to define *older adult* as forty-five and over—for the purposes of program invitations, writing this book, and engaging with communications teams about the audience. Why? To broaden the perspective. To make space for more people. To shift the narrative. Yes, it presents a challenge—there is an enormous spectrum of lived experiences, knowledge, skills, interests, and beliefs between the ages of forty-five and one-hundred-plus. But here's

the beauty: that diversity creates opportunities for shared learning, meaningful connections, and intergenerational wisdom.

I've seen a significant rise in the number and diversity of attendees at programs that implement this new mindset in our community. I've witnessed powerful moments between *younger* and *older* older adults (yes, it's a mouthful!). The depth of dialogue, the compassion, the laughter— it's richer when more voices are included.

So, here's my invitation to you:

Don't let society, or even your birth certificate, define your life stage. You can be fifty and feel ancient and irrelevant. Or you can be seventy-five and be in the best mental, physical, and spiritual shape of your life. It's all perspective.

In the end, who and what you are in this life is shaped by your intentions, your mindset, your actions—and how you choose to show up each day. Don't accept a box someone else built for you. Choose your own narrative. Choose how you want to live and age well. And do it on your terms, as your authentic self.

Because you're not just an *older adult*. You're a powerhouse of lived experience, wisdom, resilience, humor, and untapped potential.

Let's stop trying to define it—and start living it.

WWW.PHILOSOPHIAWITHIN.COM

How Your Beliefs About Aging Determine How Long and Well You Live

In **Breaking the Age Code, Becca Levy, PhD**, a researcher and professor at Yale, explores the profound impact of age beliefs on health, longevity, and well-being. Through scientific studies and real-world examples, she reveals how societal stereotypes about aging influence not only how we perceive growing older but also how our bodies and minds respond to it—and I could not agree more! **Let's collectively and positively change the narrative about aging with these key insights and takeaways:**

Age Beliefs Shape Our Health & Longevity

- People with positive perceptions of aging live an average of **7.5 years longer** than those with negative beliefs.
- Positive attitudes toward aging are linked to better physical health, memory, and emotional well-being.

The Power of the Mind-Body Connection

- Negative age stereotypes increase stress, leading to cognitive decline, cardiovascular issues, and even a higher risk of Alzheimer's.
- Positive self-perceptions about aging can improve recovery from illness, increase resilience, and promote active lifestyles.

Challenging Ageism Benefits Everyone

- Society often promotes ageist beliefs through media, workplace discrimination, and medical bias.
- When older adults reject these stereotypes, they engage more in life, pursue goals, and maintain independence.

Practical Strategies to Shift Age Beliefs

- **Awareness:** Recognizing how age stereotypes affect personal and societal attitudes.
- **Reframing Aging:** Focusing on the strengths that come with age, such as wisdom, adaptability, and experience.

- **Intergenerational Connections:** Engaging with younger generations to foster understanding and break ageist myths.
- **Media Literacy:** Challenging negative portrayals of aging in advertisements, TV, and social media.

Aging as a Time of Growth & Possibility

- Older adults contribute significantly to families, communities, and workplaces.
- Aging can be a period of new opportunities, creativity, and deep personal fulfillment.

Changing how we think about aging isn't just about attitude — it's a scientifically proven way to improve our health, extend our lives, and create a more age-inclusive society.

WWW.PHILOSOPHIAWITHIN.COM

You Could Live a Long Time: Are You Ready?

Lyndsay Green's *You Could Live a Long Time: Are You Ready?* challenges conventional retirement and aging advice by focusing on the real-life experiences of older adults who have aged well. Through interviews and research, she explores what truly contributes to a fulfilling, independent, and meaningful later life beyond just financial security. Her key insights are mirrors of daily conversations I have with older adults and seniors in my professional work, and I encourage you to consider them thoughtfully.

1. **Money Alone Won't Ensure a Good Old Age**

   - While financial planning is important, social connections, purpose, and adaptability matter just as much— if not more—for a happy and healthy old age.
   - *Many well-off seniors still feel lonely or unfulfilled, proving that wealth is not the key to contentment.*

2. **Build Strong Relationships & Social Networks**

   - Those who maintain friendships and community ties tend to age better than those who isolate.
   - Having a diverse social circle—including friends of different ages—helps combat loneliness and keeps life engaging.

3. **Independence Requires Planning & Flexibility**

   - Aging well means making conscious choices about housing, healthcare, and daily living arrangements.
   - Staying in one's home may not always be the best option—having an adaptable mindset about future living arrangements is key.

4. **Find Purpose & Meaning in Later Life**

   - Those who stay engaged in activities—whether through volunteering, mentorship, hobbies, or learning— experience greater well-being.
   - Retirement shouldn't be about withdrawing from life but about rediscovering passions and contributing in new ways.

5. **Health Is More Than Just Diet & Exercise**

   - While staying physically active is crucial, mental and emotional resilience play a significant role in longevity.
   - Having a sense of humor, staying optimistic, and continuously learning contribute to a stronger, more adaptable mindset.

6. **Let Go of Expectations & Embrace Aging**

   - Instead of fearing old age, embracing the opportunities and freedoms it brings can lead to a more enjoyable life.
   - Society often defines aging by loss - try reframing it as a period of growth and change.

Aging is about connection, purpose, and mindset rather than just financial security. By planning beyond money and prioritizing relationships, independence, and lifelong learning, we can create a fulfilling and meaningful later life.

WWW.PHILOSOPHIAWITHIN.COM

Rewiring the Mind for Wellness

In his compelling series **Rewired on Gaia**, **Dr. Joe Dispenza**[1] explores the profound connection between the mind, body, and energy field, offering insights that align perfectly with the principles of holistic wellness. His teachings emphasize the transformative power of **neuroplasticity— the brain's ability to rewire itself through focused thought, emotion, and intention.**

For older adults, families, and helping professionals, embracing these concepts offers a powerful framework for living and aging well. Dr.Dispenza explains that **our habitual thoughts and emotions create neural pathways that shape our reality**. When these patterns are negative—driven by stress, fear, or limiting beliefs—they can lead to chronic health issues, emotional stagnation, and a diminished quality of life.

However, through practices such as meditation, visualization, and breathwork, he demonstrates how **individuals can break free from old patterns** and create new, healthier neural networks. This rewiring process not only improves mental and emotional well-being but also has the potential to influence physical health by **enhancing immune function, reducing inflammation, and promoting cellular regeneration.**

For older adults, Dispenza's teachings are particularly empowering. His emphasis on the mind's capacity to influence the body challenges the notion that aging inevitably leads to decline. By consciously creating elevated emotional states—such as **gratitude, joy, and love**— individuals can activate the brain's reward centers and stimulate the release of regenerative chemicals like oxytocin and serotonin. **This process fosters resilience, vitality, and a more optimistic outlook on life, regardless of age.**

Families and helping professionals can also apply these principles by encouraging loved ones and clients to cultivate daily mindfulness practices. Techniques such as guided meditation or heart-centered breathing, inspired by Dispenza's methods, can support emotional regulation, reduce anxiety, and enhance cognitive function.

Dr. Dispenza's work in *Rewired on Gaia* offers a hopeful reminder: We are not victims of aging or circumstance. **Through intention, practice, and the willingness to shift our internal state, we have the power to promote healing, longevity, and greater fulfillment—at any stage of life.**

---

1   *Dr. Joe Dispenza is a neuroscientist, chiropractor, and bestselling author known for his work on the mind-body connection, neuroplasticity, and self-healing. He holds a doctor of chiropractic degree from Life University and blends neuroscience, epigenetics, and quantum physics to teach individuals how to rewire their brains and promote wellness through meditation and elevated emotional states.*

In *Becoming Supernatural: How Common People Are Doing the Uncommon*, Dr. Joe Dispenza presents a **synthesis of neuroscience, epigenetics, psychoneuroimmunology, quantum physics, and ancient spiritual practices to argue that individuals can intentionally influence their biology, health, and life outcomes.** Central to Dispenza's thesis is the idea that our thoughts and emotions—when properly aligned—can transcend the limitations of the physical body, habitual identity, and time-bound experiences to catalyze profound healing and personal transformation.

Dispenza's work is **grounded in empirical data collected through thousands of EEG brain scans, heart-rate variability studies, and real-time physiological monitoring** during advanced meditation workshops. He demonstrates how participants can consistently shift from high-beta brainwave states (associated with stress and survival) into theta and gamma states, which are correlated with deep meditative absorption and mystical experiences. These findings suggest transformative neuroplastic potential and emotional regulation for anyone, **particularly relevant to older adults seeking cognitive resilience and psychosocial well-being.**

Referencing the pioneering work of scientists such as Dr. Candace Pert (author of *Molecules of Emotion*) and Dr. Bruce Lipton (*The Biology of Belief*), Dispenza explores how **the body is not merely a passive recipient of external stimuli but an active participant in the cocreation of health through energetic and informational fields.** He also draws upon research from the HeartMath Institute, highlighting how **heart-brain coherence—a harmonious synchronization between the cardiovascular and nervous systems—can regulate stress hormones, enhance immune function, and support emotional well-being**. These findings are highly congruent with the principles of healthy aging, particularly in reducing chronic inflammation and enhancing overall quality of life.

A key argument throughout *Becoming Supernatural* is that sustained elevated emotions—such as **gratitude, compassion, and joy—paired with clear intentional thought can trigger measurable changes in gene expression (epigenetics), immune response, and even the perception of time and identity.** He references the work of Dr. Dawson Church (*Mind to Matter*) to support claims that conscious intention can influence measurable physiological outcomes. For older adults, caregivers, and helping professionals, Dispenza's work offers **a compelling case for integrating meditative and mindfulness-based interventions into daily routines.** Structured meditations, breathwork techniques, and energy-center-alignment practices offer practical tools for regulating the autonomic nervous system, enhancing neuroplasticity, and cultivating a future-oriented mindset—key components for those navigating later life transitions or caregiving responsibilities.

As explored in *Living & Aging Well,* **healthy aging is a multidimensional process that encompasses biological, psychological, social, and spiritual domains.** *Becoming Supernatural* enriches this perspective by offering a vision of aging not as a decline in capacities but as an opportunity to reconnect with one's deeper self and innate healing potential. Together, these works support a paradigm shift—**from passive aging to empowered living.**

How Do You Imagine Your Future?

As you look ahead to the next chapter of your life, what do you see?

Do you picture yourself traveling to new places, spending time with family, or engaging in a meaningful volunteer role?

Perhaps you envision a slower pace, focusing on hobbies, wellness, and friendships. Planning for your future means considering your health, finances, living arrangements, and how you want to spend your time.

By making thoughtful choices now—whether it's staying active, nurturing relationships, or exploring new opportunities—you can shape a fulfilling and joyful future that aligns with your values and aspirations.

Reflection Questions:

- What brings you the most joy and fulfillment in life?

- How do you want to spend your time in retirement or later years?

- Do you see yourself volunteering, mentoring, or giving back to your community?

- Would you like to travel, take up a new hobby, or continue learning?

- Where do you want to live—close to family, in a vibrant community, or in a peaceful setting?

- What steps can you take today to ensure you stay healthy, financially secure, and socially connected?

Philosophia
—— WITHIN ——

Ideas & Examples:

1. Volunteering at a community center, school, or seniors' program.

2. Becoming a mentor for younger generations or supporting local charities.

3. Taking up a creative passion like painting, music, or writing.

4. Exploring travel—whether local adventures or international trips.

5. Prioritizing health through fitness, meditation, or nutrition.

6. Building and maintaining strong friendships and family connections.

7. Considering future living arrangements that support independence and well-being.

Your future is a canvas—how do you want to paint it?

"I have the power to shape a future filled with joy, purpose, and connection. Each choice I make today brings me closer to the life I envision."

Your Future, Your Choice: Moving Forward with Confidence

If you are deciding whether to downsize, relocate, or remain in your home, remember that the right choice will balance your health, safety, and happiness.

I always encourage consideration of three pillars essential for long-term well-being and peace of mind.

Ask yourself:

✓ **AM I HEALTHY?** Can I maintain my well-being and independence where I am?

✓ **AM I SAFE?** Is my environment secure and supportive of my current and future needs?

✓ **AM I HAPPY?** Do I feel fulfilled, connected, and at ease in my living situation?

If one of these feels uncertain, it may be time to explore options that better align with your evolving needs. This is not just about change—it's about **showing yourself love and grace** as you create a future that honors your **comfort, dignity, and joy.**

You are not alone in this journey.

Seek support, take small steps, and trust that a new chapter can bring renewed possibilities. Reach out today to explore resources, connect with professionals, and take the next step toward a life that truly supports you. 💗

Ten Positive Affirmations for Embracing Change:

Philosophia WITHIN

1. I am embracing this new chapter with courage and confidence.

2. I deserve a home and environment that supports my health, safety, and happiness.

3. Letting go of the past does not mean losing the love and memories I carry in my heart.

4. I trust myself to make decisions that honor my needs and well- being.

5. I welcome support from loved ones and professionals who care about my happiness.

6. Change is an opportunity for growth, joy, and new experiences.

7. My worth is not measured by my home but by the love and wisdom I share.

8. I give myself grace as I navigate this transition at my own pace.

9. I am surrounded by love, and I am never alone in this journey.

10. My future is bright, and I look forward to the possibilities ahead.

Take a deep breath and remember: You are strong, loved, and capable of embracing this next stage of life with confidence and peace.

Common Concerns and Fears

Philosophia
— WITHIN —

 ## Family Dynamics

Loved ones may worry about making the right decision and the potential for family disagreements.

 ## Emotional Impact

The thought of leaving a longtime home filled with memories can be emotionally taxing.

 ## Quality of Care

Uncertainty about the standard of care in a new environment can cause anxiety.

 ## Financial Implications

Concerns about the affordability of new living arrangements and the potential depletion of savings are common.

 ## Loss of Independence

Seniors may fear losing autonomy and control over their daily lives.

Understanding Older Adult Abuse

Definition • Signs • Risk Factors • What You Can Do

What is Older Adult Abuse?

Older Adult Abuse is any intentional or negligent act by a caregiver or other person that causes harm or serious risk to a vulnerable older adult. It can happen in private homes, care facilities, or in public, and it often goes unreported due to fear, shame, or dependence on the abuser.

Types of Older Adult Abuse?

- **Physical Abuse:** Hitting, pushing, shaking, or using restraints inappropriately.
- **Emotional or Psychological Abuse:** Verbal insults, threats, humiliation, or isolation.
- **Financial Abuse:** Theft, fraud, misuse of funds or assets, or pressure to change legal documents.
- **Neglect:** Failing to provide necessary care, including food, medication, or hygiene.
- **Sexual Abuse:** Any unwanted or forced sexual contact or activity.
- **Spiritual or Cultural Abuse:** Denying access to spiritual practices or cultural identity.
- **Self-Neglect:** When an older adult cannot or does not care for their basic needs and safety.

Signs of Older Adult Abuse

Signs the Older Adult May Show:

- Unexplained bruises, burns, or injuries.
- Fear, anxiety, depression, or withdrawal.
- Sudden changes in financial situation.
- Poor hygiene, malnutrition, or untreated medical conditions.
- Reluctance to speak when certain people are around.
- Frequent falls or hospital visits.
- Unusual changes to wills, property, or banking.

Signs the Abusive Person May Show:

- Controlling behavior (restricting visits, calls, or access).
- Speaking for the older adult or refusing to let them speak.
- Treating the older adult like a child.
- Anger, frustration, or resentment toward caregiving.
- Financial dependence on the older adult.
- Substance misuse.
- Isolation of the older adult from family, friends, or community.

- Neglect, leaving a dependent person along for long periods of time.

Common Risk Factors for Abuse

- Social isolation or lack of community connections.
- Cognitive decline or dementia.
- History of family conflict, mental health issues or intergenerational trauma.
- Dependence of caregiver on the older adult (emotional or financial).
- Caregiver burnout or lack of support.
- Living with others who misuse substances or have a history of violence.

Common Roles of Abusers

- Adult children or grandchildren.
- Spouse or partner.
- Caregivers (formal or informal).
- Friends, neighbors, or roommates.
- Professionals or scam artists targeting vulnerable seniors.

Self-Check: Could My Behaviour Be Harmful?

Ask yourself:

- Do I speak over or for the older adult often?
- Do I feel resentful, impatient, or overwhelmed by caregiving?
- Have I borrowed money, used a card, or signed documents without permission?

- Do I withhold affection, information, or resources when I'm upset?
- Have I made decisions for the older adult without involving them?

If you answered **yes** to any of these, it may be time to seek support or guidance. Abuse can happen unintentionally when stress or power imbalances aren't appropriately managed.

What If You Suspect Abuse But the Person Denies It?

- Listen and express concern gently. Avoid judgment or pressure.
- Document what you observe. Track signs and patterns of behavior.
- Offer ongoing support. Stay present and consistent.
- Learn about reporting options. You can still report suspected abuse to Adult Protective Services or local authorities for investigation.
- In case of immediate danger, call emergency services.

If You Need Help or Want to Report Concerns:

In Canada: Call the Seniors Safety Line at 1-866-299-1011.

In the US: Call the National Elder Abuse Hotline at 1-800-677-1116.

These help lines provide counseling, safety planning, and referrals to local resources.

Or contact your local Adult Protective Services or community support office.

Abuse Prevention for Older Adults

Practical Tips for Staying Safe, Independent, and Empowered

Plan Ahead

- Make decisions while you're healthy and independent.
- Plan for future care, finances, and living arrangements.

Make a Will & Review It Annually

Update your will thoughtfully, and only after speaking with someone you trust.

Protect Your Finances

- Set up direct deposit for pensions and checks.
- Don't sign over property or assets based on promises.
- Keep control of your finances and documents as long as you're able.
- Seek reputable organizations who can assist with financial management.

Ask for Help When You Need It

There is strength—not weakness—in reaching out.

Set Healthy Boundaries

- Avoid placing expectations on your children without their agreement.
- Think carefully before allowing adult children to move back in. Seek advice if unsure.

Stay Involved

- Remain active in your community.
- Build friendships across generations.
- Don't rely solely on family for social life or support.

Know Your Rights

Never let age stop you from speaking up or accessing services.

Protect Your Home & Belongings

- Safeguard valuables; make your home secure.
- Don't leave cash or important items unattended.

Be Cautious with Promises

Never give away your home or assets in exchange for care without legal advice.

Stay Informed

Learn about elder abuse signs and resources.

Trust your instincts—if something feels wrong, speak to someone.

Abuse Prevention for Families and Helping Professionals

Supporting Older Adults with Respect, Awareness, and Compassion

Have the Conversation Early

- Discuss wishes for future care before a crisis happens—include preferences for medical treatment, daily living, and end-of-life care.

Encourage Legal Planning

- Help them create a power of attorney and personal directive while they're well. These documents protect their rights and ensure their voice is heard.

Be Realistic About Caregiving

- Assess your ability to provide care—physically, emotionally, and financially.
- Your well-being matters too.

Seek Support & Share Responsibility

- Talk openly with other family members about caregiving roles.
- Ask for help, respite, and support in ways that work for everyone.

Respect Privacy & Boundaries

- All relationships need balance—honor time alone and time together.
- Create respectful spaces for all members of the household.

Plan—Don't React

- Avoid taking in a parent or relative during a crisis without discussion and agreement from all affected family members.

Let Go of Guilt

- Choosing a care facility or alternative support does not mean failure—it means doing what's best for everyone.

Understand the Environment

- Evaluate whether your home is physically safe and emotionally supportive.
- Don't assume that past family tensions will disappear by cohabiting.

Stay Informed & Connected

- Learn about community resources available to older adults and caregivers.
- Don't hesitate to use them—they exist to help.

Know the Signs

- Recognize caregiver burnout and address it early.
- Stay alert to signs of elder abuse—emotional, physical, financial, or neglect.
- Speak up, advocate, and always listen with empathy.

Keep Humor & Heart

- A little laughter and love can go a long way. Be patient—with your loved one and yourself.

WWW.PHILOSOPHIAWITHIN.COM

What to Do If You Think You Are Being Abused

It's crucial to ensure that any decision regarding an older adult's living situation is made freely and without undue influence. Abuse can take many forms, including **physical, emotional, financial, or neglect, and is most often committed by a family member or a trusted person.**

Leave the situation if you are in immediate danger.

Go to a safe place, such as with a neighbour, friend, or relative. Go into a business, or when calling a helpline, ask to be taken to a shelter. If you are unable to leave your home, call 911 immediately.

Confide in someone you trust and tell them about what is happening.

This could be a friend or family member, public health nurse, social worker, home care worker, someone at your place of worship, or a doctor. If it is an emergency, call 911 or your local law enforcement.

Keep a record.

Write down what is happening to you and keep a daily record. This will help you to document the abuse and help others assist you if you need it.

Take legal action.

All forms of abuse are wrong. Some forms are illegal. You may want to think about a court protection order that would stop the abusive person from having contact with you. Your local police service or a police-based victim services unit can give you information.

Don't blame yourself

No one deserves to be abused. It is not your fault, and help is available. Many groups in your community want to help you protect your rights, safety, and dignity.

The Emotional Side of Downsizing and Moving

The decision to move, downsize, or age in place is often one of the most difficult choices a senior will face. It's not just about logistics—it's about emotions, memories, and identity.

Common Emotional Challenges & Barriers to Letting Go of a Home Full of Memories

The home represents years of experiences, milestones, and personal history.

☀ Fear of Change

Moving to a new environment means stepping into the unknown.

☀ Loss of Independence

Accepting that assistance is needed can feel like a loss of control or feel embarassing.

☀ Decision Overload

Sorting through belongings, deciding what to keep, and coordinating a move is often overwhelming and may hinder decision making.

☀ Financial Concerns

Worrying about the cost of moving and future expenses can feel overwhelming and, sometimes debilitating.

☀ Guilt & Family Expectations

Feeling pressure from family or guilt about leaving a home that may have been in the family for generations may cause physical or emotional symptoms and, feel overwhelming.

Philosophia
— WITHIN —

Have a Positive Outlook

☀ See the Opportunities in Change

Downsizing can free up time, energy, and financial resources for new experiences. A fresh start can bring renewed joy. A new space can mean less maintenance, more safety, and new social connections.

☀ Your Memories Are Not Tied to a Place

Cherished moments live in your heart, not in a house. Memories will go with you wherever you go.

☀ You Are in Control

Choosing to move before a crisis gives you the power to make decisions that are best for you. It's okay to feel emotional—acknowledge your feelings and allow yourself time to process them. Seek support—talk to a counselor, trusted friends, or family members about your fears and hopes.

☀ Process Emotions & Make a Decision

- **Journal Your Thoughts** – Writing can help clarify emotions and priorities.
- **Talk It Out** – Share your concerns with family, friends, or a professional.

- **Create a Memory Book** – Take photos of your home and special belongings before letting them go.
- **Visit New Living Options** – Touring potential homes can ease anxiety by making the transition feel real and exciting.
- **Make a Pros and Cons List** – Writing down benefits and drawbacks can help you see the situation more clearly.
- **Take Small Steps** – Declutter one room at a time to ease into the process.

Philosophia
WITHIN

Tips for Discussions About Living and Aging Decisions with Family Members

 Respectfully engaging in conversations about changing a senior's living situation, whether due to health concerns or proactive long-term planning, requires sensitivity, empathy, and active listening by everyone involved.

Here are some simple yet effective guidelines to facilitate these discussions.

Timing & Transparency

Choose the Right Time and Place: Select a comfortable, private setting free from distractions to ensure everyone feels at ease.

Be Open and Honest: Encourage all participants to express their thoughts and feelings openly. Transparency fosters trust and understanding.

Patience & Respect

Be Patient and Respectful: Understand that these conversations can be challenging for all. Allow time for reflection and avoid rushing decisions.

Ask Open-Ended Questions: Encourage deeper discussion by asking questions that require more than a yes/no answer, such as, "How do you feel about exploring new living arrangements?"

Active Listening

Give Full Attention: Listen without interrupting, showing respect for the speaker's perspective.

Reflect and Clarify: Paraphrase what has been said to ensure understanding and ask clarifying questions when necessary.

Acknowledge Emotions: Recognize and validate the emotions expressed, showing empathy and support.

Focus on Shared Goals

Emphasize common objectives, such as safety, health, and quality of life, to align everyone's intentions.

Ask questions like: "How will my decisions effect those I am connected to?"

Ways Family and Helpers Can Be Supportive

Philosophia
— WITHIN —

 ### Listen Without Judgment

Acknowledge their feelings. Validate their fears, sadness, or hesitation rather than dismissing them. Allow them to express their emotions without rushing them to decide. Be respectful.

 ### Encourage but Don't Push

Emphasize the benefits: less stress, more social opportunities, a safer environment. Provide information and options but respect their timeline. Be patient.

 ### Help with Small Tasks

Offer to assist with decluttering, researching options, or packing.

 ### Reassure & Stay Involved

Family plays a crucial role in helping a loved one through the decision to move or age in place. If they fear isolation, remind them you'll stay connected and visit regularly, if that's a possibility.

Be Considerate of Family & Helpers

Moving or aging well at home will impact family members and helpers, **especially those who are still working or raising a family**.

Here's how seniors can be mindful of their loved ones' time and energy.

 ## Acknowledge & Be Open

Express gratitude and recognize the effort they put into helping—often. Have honest conversations about how much help they can realistically provide.

 ## Plan & Communicate Early

Making decisions in advance prevents last-minute stress for family members. Understand that family members have their own responsibilities and may not always be available.

 ## Consider & Care

Encourage Self-Care—Let family members know you appreciate their help but also encourage them to take care of themselves. Consider professional help—Hiring movers, organizers, or legal professionals who can reduce the burden on your family.

Rights and Respect Statements

 Family & Helpers

As a caregiver, I recognize my dedication and compassion, and I honor my own well-being in the process. I affirm these rights for myself with grace, respect, wisdom, balance, and self-love—free from guilt.

1. I have the right to care for myself with the same love and attention I give to others.
2. I have the right to set boundaries without guilt, knowing that my well-being matters.
3. I have the right to ask for and accept help, understanding that I am not meant to do this alone.
4. I have the right to rest and recharge, knowing that renewal strengthens my ability to care.
5. I have the right to experience joy and fulfillment beyond my caregiving role.
6. I have the right to express my emotions—including frustration, sadness, and exhaustion—without judgment.
7. I have the right to make mistakes and learn from them with kindness toward myself.
8. I have the right to prioritize my own health, physically, emotionally, and spiritually.
9. I have the right to say no to unrealistic expectations and unnecessary burdens.
10. I have the right to celebrate my dedication and recognize that I am doing enough.

I honor myself as I honor others. I give myself permission to care with strength and love—without sacrificing my own well-being.

Older Adults/Seniors

As I age, I honor my wisdom, dignity, and the life I have built. I affirm my right to live with grace, respect, balance, and self-love—free from guilt or limitation.

1. I have the right to live with dignity and be treated with kindness, patience, and respect.

2. I have the right to make my own decisions and have them honored, even if I'm deemed incapable.

3. I have the right to ask for and receive support without feeling like a burden.

4. I have the right to set boundaries and choose what is best for my well-being.

5. I have the right to stay engaged in life, pursue my passions, and continue learning and growing.

6. I have the right to express my emotions freely and be heard without judgment.

7. I have the right to prioritize my physical, emotional, and spiritual health.

8. I have the right to feel safe in my home, relationships, and community.

9. I have the right to say no to anything that does not serve my well-being.

10. I have the right to celebrate my life, my experiences, and my worth—at every stage of aging.

I embrace this chapter of life with strength, joy, and the knowledge that I am valued, loved, and enough.

Thriving in Later Life: A Call to Empower and Honor Older Adults

In the aftermath of the COVID-19 pandemic, communities around the world have been called to reflect on and improve the experiences of older adults. This turning point presents a powerful opportunity to address long- standing challenges, embrace forward-thinking solutions, and issue an urgent call to create environments in which older adults can truly thrive—mentally, physically, emotionally, and spiritually.

A Holistic Approach to Aging

Aging well is not merely about extending life but enriching it in every possible way. The pandemic underscored critical issues affecting older adults, including social isolation, healthcare accessibility, and financial insecurity. However, true wellness extends beyond these concerns. It requires an approach that nurtures mental clarity, emotional resilience, physical vitality, and spiritual fulfillment.

A notable trend is the rise of "solo aging," where individuals navigate later life without immediate family support. This demographic shift necessitates robust community engagement, comprehensive financial planning, and proactive healthcare advocacy to ensure that solo agers maintain a high quality of life.

Reimagining the Role of Older Adults in Society

It is time to shift the narrative that older adults are no longer valuable to society simply because they may not be in the workforce. Instead, we must recognize and celebrate their vast contributions. Older adults have the gift of time—a priceless resource that can be invested in personal growth, creative expression, and meaningful service to others. They are artists, storytellers, historians, mentors, and advisors who bring wisdom and depth to communities, families, and leadership structures.

Progressive Initiatives Enhancing Older Adult Care

The COVID-19 pandemic exposed significant gaps in the care of older adults, prompting innovative responses worldwide. One such initiative is the Program of All-Inclusive Care for the Elderly (PACE) in the United States. PACE organizations rapidly adapted during the pandemic by shifting from primarily center-based to home- based models of care. They increased in-home services, leveraged telehealth, and implemented infection prevention efforts, demonstrating a commitment to person-centered, integrated care that empowers older adults to remain in their preferred residential settings.[2]

Additionally, adult day centers have evolved into multicultural hubs catering to the diverse needs of older adults. For instance, the Sunshine Adult Day Center in New Jersey provides culturally enriching environments that emphasize mental and physical wellness, aiming to prevent nursing home admissions. These centers offer activities tailored to participants' cultural backgrounds, fostering a sense of community and belonging.[3]

Lessons from the Pandemic: Identified Gaps and Future Preparedness

The pandemic highlighted critical deficiencies in emergency planning, infection control, and staffing within aged-care facilities. In Victoria, Australia, for example, COVID-19 outbreaks in 2020 led to over six-hundred resident deaths, revealing severe shortcomings in the aged care sector. Families of affected individuals have expressed frustration over the lack of accountability and fear that critical issues, such as reliance on casual staff and understaffing, remain unresolved.[4]

To address these gaps and prepare for future health crises, several measures are recommended:

Improving Access to Care: Ensuring that older adults have access to affordable and quality long-term care services is paramount. Across twenty-two European, Organisation for Economic Co-operation and Development (OECD) countries, close to 40 percent of people with difficulties in household activities or personal care reported unmet needs for help. Addressing these gaps requires better data collection to evaluate service effectiveness and efficiency.[5]

Enhancing Quality Standards: Developing comprehensive quality frameworks that focus on both inputs and outcomes is essential. This includes measuring staff interaction time with care recipients, improvements in functioning, and patient-reported outcomes. Publicly available quality indicators can improve transparency and accountability in care services.[6]

Strengthening Workforce Measures: Attracting and retaining skilled care workers is critical. Effective strategies include improving on-the-job training, raising wages, promoting a healthier work environment, and implementing organizational improvements such as self-managed

2   ScienceDirect+1PubMed+1 https://www.sciencedirect.com/science/article/pii/S1525861023009817?utm_source=chatgpt.com

3   AP News https://apnews.com/article/98943152ebfc62dd898262d93ca32e6f?utm_source=chatgpt.com

4   Herald Sun https://www.heraldsun.com.au/news/victoria/doomed-to-repeat-history-fears-covid-aged-care-outbreak-issues-still-not-fixed/news-story/87e2e9acc532e493f727bedcbc9a025c?utm_source=chatgpt.com

5   AARP International https://www.aarpinternational.org/the-journal/current-edition/journal-articles-blog/2023/08/atj2023-colombo-suzuki?utm_source=chatgpt.com

6   AARP International https://www.aarpinternational.org/the-journal/current-edition/journal-articles-blog/2023/08/atj2023-colombo-suzuki?utm_source=chatgpt.com

teams. Countries like Japan have successfully recruited workers from sectors with decreasing labor demand, demonstrating the potential of targeted recruitment policies.[7]

From "Aging in Place" to "Living and Aging Well"

The traditional concept of "aging in place"—remaining in one's home as one ages—may not always align with an individual's needs for safety, health, or overall well-being. It is imperative to shift the dialogue toward "living and aging well", a holistic approach that prioritizes quality of life, irrespective of living arrangements. This perspective encourages older adults to choose environments that best support their well-being, whether at home, in a communal setting, or elsewhere.

Empowering Change: Advocacy and Leadership

To effect meaningful change, individuals can take active roles as changemakers and leaders in the following ways:

Community Engagement: Participate in local organizations that support older adults, helping to foster inclusive communities that value their contributions.

Policy Advocacy: Advocate for policies that address the needs of older adults, such as improved healthcare services, affordable housing, and social programs that combat isolation.

Education and Awareness: Challenge ageism by promoting positive narratives about aging and highlighting the diverse experiences and capabilities of older adults.

Older adults themselves can advocate for their needs by:

Self-Advocacy: Clearly communicating their preferences and requirements to family members, caregivers, and healthcare providers.

Lifelong Learning: Engaging in educational opportunities to stay informed about their rights and the resources available to them.

Peer Support: Building networks with fellow older adults to share experiences, offer mutual support, and collectively voice concerns.

Elevating Respect and Appreciation

At the heart of improving the experience of older adults is a societal shift toward greater respect, value, and appreciation for their diverse lived experiences and wisdom. It is time to celebrate aging as an honor rather than a decline. I invite older adults to wear their white or gray hair proudly as a "crown of wisdom", a visible sign of the knowledge and life experience

---

7   AARP International https://www.aarpinternational.org/the-journal/current-edition/journal-articles-blog/2023/08/atj2023-colombo-suzuki?utm_source=chatgpt.com

they bring to their communities. Their voices should not only be heard but sought after in discussions that shape the future.

Language plays a crucial role in this transformation. Terms like *older adult* are preferred over *senior* or *elderly,* as they convey respect and avoid negative stereotypes. The American Geriatrics Society emphasizes that language should reflect the dignity and contributions of older individuals, advocating for the use of *older adult* to promote a more inclusive and respectful discourse.[8]

A Call to Action

As we navigate the post-COVID world, let us commit to creating societies that honor and uplift older adults. This endeavor requires collective effort, compassion, and a steadfast dedication to valuing every stage of life. By addressing common concerns, embracing progressive initiatives, and fostering environments of respect and appreciation, we can ensure that individuals not only age **but truly thrive.**

WWW.PHILOSOPHIAWITHIN.COM

---

8   AGS Journal, (2024). https://agsjournals.onlinelibrary.wiley.com/doi/full/10.1111/jgs.14941?utm_source= chatgpt.com

Let's Learn

Asking questions, hearing impactful stories of innovation, gathering helpful information, and reviewing common and creative options with these practical tools will help you plan your ideal older years.

"Aging intentionally means embracing knowledge, exploring possibilities, and shaping a future that reflects my heart and soul. By seeking information and exploring innovation, I am actively creating a life of independence, vitality, and purpose."

– My Soul

Should I Move?

 ## Living & Aging Well at Home

Successful aging at home means having the necessary services, healthcare, and social supports to continue living safely and independently in your home or community for as long as possible. If you are a senior or approaching retirement and want to explore what steps you can take to prepare for the future, this guide is for you.

Thinking ahead and planning proactively can help you maintain control over your decisions and make the most of your later years. By creating a plan now, you can increase your chances of aging comfortably and confidently in a way that aligns with your needs and preferences.

 ## To Move or Not to Move

This guide includes checklists to help you assess your current plan, if you have one, and identify steps you can take now to enhance your well-being as you age. It is informed by the experiences of seniors who have thoughtfully prepared for their later years.

Consider what you want your life to look like in five, fifteen, or twenty years and what actions you can take today to help you stay independent and prepared for any changes ahead. Having a well- thought-out plan can reduce the risk of making rushed decisions in response to a crisis.

By planning for the future now, you can help ensure you live the life you want in the years to come.

Proactive Planning Benefits and Risks

☀ Benefits of Proactive Planning

- Greater independence, security, and quality of life.
- Ability to make informed choices that align with your needs and preferences.
- Control over where and how you live as you age.
- Better financial management and stability.
- Access to support systems before challenges arise.

Philosophia
— WITHIN —

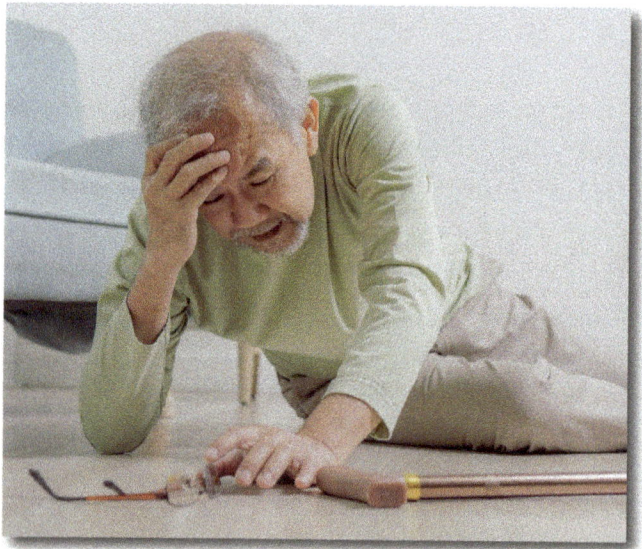

☀ Risks of Not Planning

- Financial strain and unexpected costs.
- Limited housing options and lack of accessibility.
- Reduced independence, leading to greater reliance on family or emergency services.
- Difficulties securing long-term care or managing medical needs.
- Rushed decisions in a crisis, reducing choices and control.

Take action now. Thoughtful planning now will provide peace of mind and greater stability in the years ahead.

Innovations in Aging Well Living Options

a small staff. Each house operates as a nonprofit charity, supported and owned by community volunteers. Abbeyfield is nondenominational and inclusive of all backgrounds.

 ## Dementia Village - Netherlands

The Hogeweyk® revolutionized dementia care in the Netherlands, inspiring a global shift toward more human- centered approaches. Rooted in deinstitutionalization and social inclusion, it reimagines traditional nursing homes as vibrant neighborhoods where residents live in shared houses based on lifestyle preferences. With access to a pub, restaurant, theater, supermarket, and clubs, the Hogeweyk fosters engagement, dignity, and autonomy. This model prioritizes possibilities over limitations, supported by trained professionals, and demonstrates a transformative vision for dementia care.

Abbeyfield Houses - Canada

Abbeyfield provides affordable housing and companionship for lonely elders within their community. Small groups of residents live together in converted houses, each managed by a house manager. Residents have private rooms, while meals and housekeeping are provided in shared spaces by

Home Share Pilot - Canada

Toronto HomeShare connects older adults (fifty-five-plus) with postsecondary students seeking affordable housing. In exchange for reduced rent ($400–600/month), students provide five to seven hours of companionship or light housework weekly.

Social workers facilitate matches, conduct screenings, and offer ongoing support. This program helps seniors age in place while providing students with affordable housing.

Multigenerational Program - Finland

Rudolf Seniors Home in Helsinki launched Finland's first multigenerational housing project in 2015 as part of A Home that Fits, funded by the city and the European Social Fund. To address youth homelessness and senior isolation, three studio rooms were offered to young adults (ages eighteen to twenty-five) in exchange for five weekly hours of social interaction with seniors. Activities like baking and music fostered meaningful connections, inspiring similar initiatives in four other Finnish cities and growing international interest.

Indigenous Elders Lodge - Canada

Construction of the Kikinow Elders Lodge is underway in Greenview, Alberta. The twelve-unit lodge will provide affordable, culturally supportive housing for Indigenous Elders, allowing them to remain in their community. The project, funded by $2.3 million from federal and provincial governments, along with contributions from the Municipal District of Greenview and the Evergreens Foundation, highlights a collaborative approach to meet the housing needs of Indigenous seniors. The lodge is expected to be completed by early 2025.

Mixed Use Developments - USA

Aegis Gardens – Newcastle, Washington opened in 2018, Aegis Gardens is a senior living community designed as a Chinese cultural hub. The five-story, mixed- use development features 131 units and integrates feng shui principles. It offers multigenerational programming (preschool, mahjong, theater), wellness services (tai chi, spa, traditional medicine), social activities (lectures, dining, events), and public trails. Developers saw mixed-use not as a challenge but as an opportunity.

Village to Village Network - USA

Villages are community-based nonprofits where neighbors support each other in aging at home. They provide social connections and essential services like transportation, home maintenance, wellness programs, and technology support. Member-driven and often volunteer-run, Villages reduce isolation, promote independence, and connect seniors with affordable, vetted resources. Originating with Beacon Hill Village in Boston, the Village Movement offers a cost- effective, community-driven approach to aging in place.

Homes For Heroes - Canada

Homes For Heroes Foundation (H4HF) provides supportive housing for veterans through dedicated Veterans' Villages. On-site caseworkers offer personalized reintegration support, including counseling, group therapy, and tailored programs.

Partnering with Veterans Affairs Canada and local agencies, H4HF helps veterans overcome challenges, achieve stability, find employment, and live independently.

Nordic Independent Living Challenge

The Nordic Independent Living Challenge was a collaboration among the five Nordic capitals—Copenhagen, Helsinki, Oslo, Reykjavík, and Stockholm—aimed at developing solutions to help the older adults and people with disabilities live independently at home. Run by Nordic Innovation, the competition attracted over four hundred innovators and narrowed down to twenty-five semi- finalists after a multistage development process. In June 2016, five finalists competed for three prizes. The challenge led to the creation of several successful companies, including Assistep, Motiview, and Siren Care, which have since expanded globally.

Retiring on a Cruise Ship

Retiring on a cruise ship is an increasingly popular option for seniors seeking a lifestyle of adventure, comfort, and convenience. Cruise lines offer all-inclusive packages, providing seniors with housing, meals, entertainment, and access to global destinations while enjoying a community-like atmosphere. This unique retirement choice allows for continuous travel, social engagement, and a carefree lifestyle, all with the amenities of a luxury resort, making it an appealing alternative to traditional retirement living.

Multigenerational - Netherlands

In Beekmos, Netherlands, a multigenerational housing initiative brings together seniors and young women, including mothers and adolescent girls, in a unique partnership between two nonprofits. The housing project, developed by Habion and Stichting Timon, features seventeen units in an urban setting close to schools and services. Seniors living on the ground floor serve as "coaches" to the young women in the remaining units, offering support in daily needs, relationship building, and social connections. Communal spaces and activities foster a strong sense of community, helping both seniors and young women improve their social skills and networks.

Innovative Architectural Design - Australia

Out-of-the-box thinking in architectural design for older adult living spaces fosters environments that prioritize independence, social connection, and well-being. By integrating accessible design elements, communal spaces, and proximity to amenities, architects can create adaptable, inclusive communities that support aging with dignity.

Innovative approaches ensure that older adults remain active, engaged, and connected, promoting both physical and emotional health. These forward-thinking designs offer a more holistic and empowering living experience for seniors.

Innovations in Assistive Technology

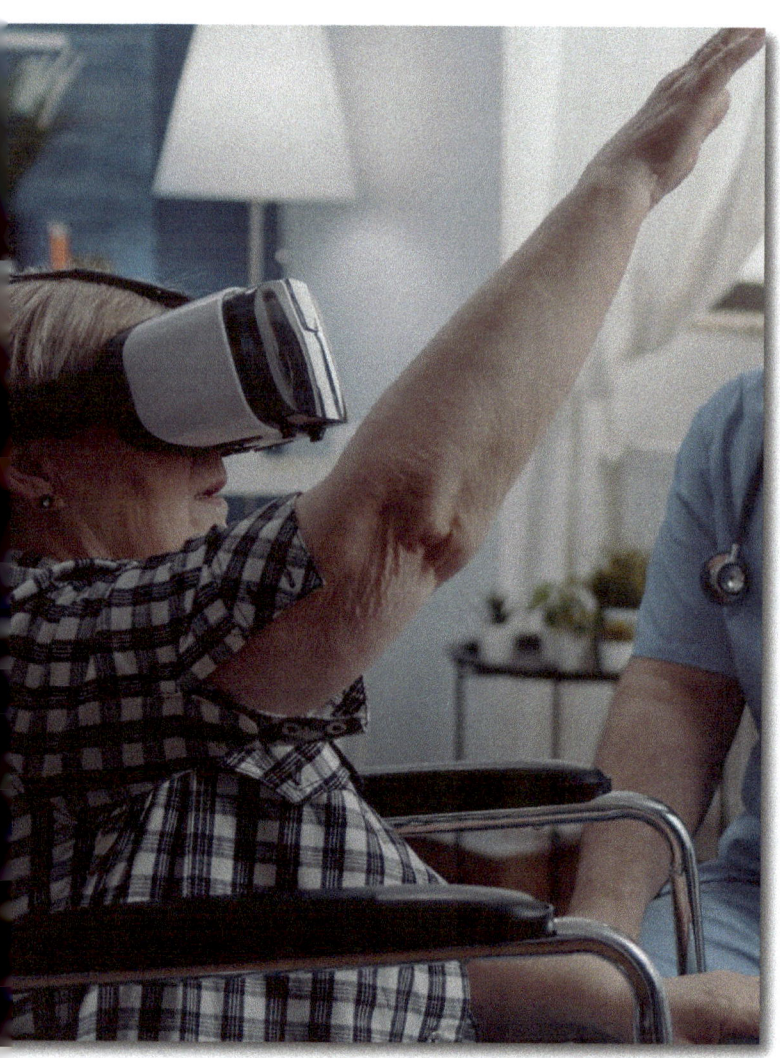

For example, *Nordic Innovation's Real Challenge* highlights solutions like smart homes with automated features, wearable health monitors, and AI-powered virtual companions that provide support and reduce isolation. Emerging technologies such as *ElliQ*, an AI-powered companion robot designed to support older adults' emotional and cognitive well-being, are offering new frontiers in care.

Additionally, platforms like *CarePredict* use AI and wearable devices to detect subtle changes in seniors' daily routines, allowing for early intervention and improved health outcomes. As these technologies continue to evolve, they hold the promise of greater autonomy, safety, and connection—empowering individuals to live fuller, more independent lives.

Here are several additional examples of emerging assistive technologies designed to enhance independence, safety, and quality of life for individuals with cognitive and physical impairments, as well as older adults and seniors:

 ## Cognitive and Memory Support

Reminder and Scheduling Devices: Tools like *MemoClock* and *Reminder Rosie* provide voice reminders for medication, appointments, and daily tasks, helping individuals with memory loss stay organized and independent.

Advancements in assistive technologies are transforming the lives of individuals with cognitive and physical impairments, as well as older adults and seniors, enabling them to maintain independence and enjoy a higher quality of life for longer. From AI-powered solutions that enhance communication and safety to groundbreaking brain implants that restore mobility, these innovations are redefining what's possible.

AI-Powered Cognitive Assistants: Devices such as *Rendever* use virtual reality (VR) to combat social isolation and stimulate cognitive function by immersing older adults in familiar or new environments, boosting mental engagement.

Brain-Computer Interfaces (BCIs): Innovations like *Synchron* allow individuals with severe physical impairments to control devices (e.g., communication tools or prosthetics) using their brain signals, improving autonomy.

 ## Mobility and Physical Assistance

Exoskeletons and Wearable Robotics: Devices such as *Ekso Bionics* provide powered support to help individuals with mobility impairments walk and move with greater ease and stability.

Smart Walkers and Canes: The *iWalkActive* is a GPS- enabled walker with fall detection and navigation assistance, helping older adults move safely and confidently.

Stair-Climbing Wheelchairs: Innovative wheelchairs like the *Scewo Bro* can climb stairs and navigate uneven terrain, expanding mobility options for individuals with physical disabilities.

 ## Vision and Hearing Aids

Smart Glasses for the Visually Impaired: Devices like *Envision Glasses* use AI to read text, recognize objects, and describe surroundings, enhancing independence for those with vision loss.

AI-Powered Hearing Aids: Products such as *Oticon More* use deep neural networks to process and filter background noise, offering clearer hearing and reducing cognitive strain.

 ## Safety and Fall Prevention

Fall Detection and Prevention Systems: Devices like *SafelyYou* use AI-powered cameras to detect falls in real time and alert caregivers, reducing response time and improving outcomes.

Smart Flooring and Mats: Technologies like Tarkett's Smart Flooring monitor gait and detect unusual movements, helping prevent falls before they occur.

 ## Smart Home and Automation

Voice-Activated Smart Assistants: Systems like *Amazon Alexa* and *Google Nest* help older adults control lighting, temperature, and security through voice commands, making daily tasks more accessible.

Automated Medication Dispensers: Devices such as *Hero* automatically dispense medication on schedule and send alerts to caregivers, preventing missed doses.

Home Monitoring Systems: Platforms like *Care Angel* use AI to check in on seniors via voice calls, providing companionship and wellness monitoring.

☀ Health and Wellness Monitoring

Wearable Health Trackers: Devices such as *Apple Watch* and *Fitbit* monitor heart rate, activity, and sleep patterns, providing early warnings of health issues.

Remote Patient Monitoring (RPM): Solutions like *Medtronic's CareLink* allow healthcare providers to monitor patients' vital signs remotely, improving chronic disease management and reducing hospital visits.

AI-Powered Diagnostic Tools: Systems like *KardiaMobile* offer personal EKGs, allowing individuals to detect atrial fibrillation and other heart conditions at home.

☀ Communication and Social Connection

AI-Powered Companion Robots: Devices such as *Jibo* and *Intuition Robotics's ElliQ* provide companionship, conversation, and reminders, reducing loneliness and supporting mental well-being.

Telepresence Robots: Tools like *Ohmni* allow remote family members or caregivers to virtually visit and interact with older adults, providing a stronger sense of connection.

Augmented and Virtual Reality for Social Engagement: Platforms like *MyndVR* use VR experiences to transport seniors to meaningful or nostalgic places, promoting emotional well-being and cognitive stimulation.

These technologies are rapidly evolving, offering promising solutions that enhance independence, promote safety, and improve the overall quality of life for individuals navigating aging or living with physical and cognitive impairments.

WWW.PHILOSOPHIAWITHIN.COM

Small Town - Big Impacts: Innovative Interactive Technology Enhancing Older Adult Well-Being

Aging well is not just about adding years to life—it's about adding life to years. As the author of *Living and Aging Well* and the initiator of this 2025-2026 project, I have always believed that aging should be a dynamic and enriching experience. In *Morinville, Alberta*, I was fortunate to bring this belief to life through a community-driven initiative that embraces innovative technology, intergenerational collaboration, and strong local partnerships to enhance the well-being of older adults and seniors. At the heart of this initiative is the *OmiVista Mobii Interactive Projection System*, a remarkable tool provided by *Sensory One*.

This interactive technology offers visually and audibly engaging activities that respond to even the smallest gestures. Whether projected onto tables or floors, the system encourages movement, stimulates cognitive functions, and fosters social interactions. For seniors, particularly those with dementia or reduced mobility, these interactive experiences provide an opportunity to reconnect with their surroundings, engage in meaningful activities, unlock memories, improve cognition, increase mobility and enhance their overall quality of life.

A Collaborative Effort for Greater Impact

What makes this project truly special is the collaborative spirit that sustains it. As a part-time adult and senior programmer with Morinville's *Family & Community Support Services (FCSS)*, I had the privilege of working alongside three seniors residences. This initiative is about the community coming together to create something meaningful for our seniors. Beyond the technology, the program thrives because of the dedication of volunteers across generations. From family members to students and caregivers, volunteers play a vital role in setting up activities, guiding seniors, and gathering feedback. Volunteerism is a key aspect of healthy aging, and I have been inspired by the way seniors support one another and offer their input towards activities within this project.

☀ Empowering Seniors and Promoting Inclusion

One of my biggest hopes for this project was that it would be inclusive and accessible to all. I am especially grateful that we have been able to engage Indigenous seniors and ensure that marginalized groups feel welcomed and valued. By making the program mobile, we have been able to bring these interactive experiences directly to seniors living in supportive housing in rural communities. Seeing the joy and engagement this has brought to people who might otherwise feel isolated has been deeply fulfilling. None of this would have been possible without federal and municipal government support. Thanks to a $25,000 grant from the New Horizons for Seniors Program, we were able to purchase the *OmiVista Mobii projector* and support marketing efforts. Once the grant project is complete, this technology will be made available for community groups to borrow, offering endless opportunities to support and enhance their programs for years to come.

☀ The Power of One Person to Spark Change

It is humbling to see how one idea, supported by passionate people, can grow into something that enriches so many lives. My hope is that this project serves as a reminder that aging well is not just about avoiding decline; it is about staying engaged, fostering connections, and embracing new experiences. I am grateful to be part of a community that values its seniors and is willing to innovate to support them, and I look forward to seeing how it continues to evolve and inspire others.

WWW.PHILOSOPHIAWITHIN.COM

Small Town - Big Impacts:
Men Building Up Men & Community

Men's Shed members - Cecil Mackesey & Montgomery Johnson during a coffee meet-up.

In my part-time capacity as the family & community supports services adult and senior programmer for the Town of Morinville in 2024, I saw a growing need for men to connect in meaningful ways and a lack of activities or programs to meet their needs and interests. **Many men, particularly during life transitions such as retirement, unemployment, or loss of a spouse, experience isolation and struggle to maintain social connections.** From this need, the Morinville Sturgeon Men's Shed Club was born—a space where men eighteen and older can gather, tinker, and share conversation while forming strong support networks.

A Men's Shed is much more than a workshop. It provides an environment where men can socialize, learn new skills, and contribute to community projects. **Research has shown that social engagement and purposeful activities significantly improve mental health, reducing stress, depression, and feelings of loneliness.** The Men's Shed helps men develop a sense of belonging, which is essential for their emotional well-being.

Since forming in April 2024, with the support of provincial and international Men's Sheds organizations, this industrious group of male volunteers have built birdhouses, cornhole games, and bottle collection bins for the Rotary Club. They've celebrated International Men's Day with dinner and football, participated in the Senior's Symposium in Gibbons, and held music jam sessions. These activities not only provide entertainment and purpose but also encourage open discussions about mental health, **breaking down the stigma around seeking support.** Currently, their founding group consists of nearly twenty men ranging in age from thirty to ninety years old.

In 2025, with the assistance of many community supporters, such as local fire and law enforcement, they are constructing a dedicated workshop at the Sturgeon Agriplex Society complex, allowing for larger projects and expanded programming. They aim to introduce photography workshops, rotating compost bin construction for the Morinville Community Gardens, and a CPR and men's mental health course. In the meantime, regular coffee gatherings at Higher

Grounds, a local volunteer-run coffee shop will continue, ensuring men have a place to connect on a casual basis. The support of Sturgeon County, the Town of Morinville, and the Rotary Club has been instrumental in making these initiatives possible.

Small towns can create big impacts. Men's Shed members aren't just building projects— they're building friendships, resilience, and stronger communities. By fostering social connections and providing a safe, welcoming environment, the Men's Shed helps men maintain their mental health while making meaningful contributions.

For more information, contact them at *morstumensshed@gmail.com* or visit the International Men's Shed Organisation at *menshed.com* to get support with starting a Men's Shed in your community.

WWW.PHILOSOPHIAWITHIN.COM

A Message from Community Partners

"Being part of the Morinville Sturgeon Men's Shed Club has been one of the most personally rewarding experiences of my life. As a veteran and community volunteer, I've long believed in the power of connection—but the Men's Shed has shown me just how vital that connection is, especially for men navigating life transitions like retirement or loss. Since joining the founding group in 2024, I've seen firsthand how this space empowers men to not only build projects but build friendships, confidence, and community. Whether we're crafting birdhouses, sharing stories over coffee, or talking openly about mental health, the Shed gives us purpose and belonging. It's more than a workshop—it's a lifeline. I truly believe small towns like ours can create big impacts, and the Men's Shed is proof of that."

— Montgomery Johnson, CD, Veteran, Past President & Community Services Leader, Rotary Club of Morinville Sturgeon; Board Member, Morinville Sturgeon Men's Shed Club

Planning the Timing of Your Move

The benefits and challenges of moving into a retirement residence before selling a home:

Philosophia
— WITHIN —

 BENEFITS

✓ **Secures a Spot in a Preferred Facility** – Many retirement homes have long waitlists, and when a spot opens, you may have to act quickly. Moving in first ensures you don't miss the opportunity.

✓ **Reduces Pressure & Stress** – Settling into a new home before selling the old one allows for a smoother transition without the urgency of immediate home sales.

✓ **Ability to Test the Fit** – Moving first allows seniors to experience the facility and determine if it meets their needs before making permanent decisions.

✓ **Easier to Sell an Empty Home** – A vacant home can be staged more effectively, making it more appealing to buyers. Additionally, showings can be scheduled without disruption.

✓ **More Time to Downsize Thoughtfully** – Without the pressure of an imminent move, seniors can take their time sorting through belongings and making decisions about what to keep, donate, or sell.

✓ **Improved Health & Safety** – If health or mobility is a concern, moving sooner provides immediate access to care, meals, and social activitwies, improving overall well-being.

 CHALLENGES

• **Financial Strain** – Paying for a retirement residence while still covering homeownership costs (mortgage, taxes, maintenance, utilities) can be costly.

• **Potential Delays in Selling** – The housing market can be unpredictable, and a longer-than-expected selling process could add financial stress.

• **Emotional Impact** – Leaving a longtime home before fully processing the transition may feel overwhelming or rushed.

• **Logistics of Managing an Empty Home** – If the home remains unsold, arrangements need to be made for maintenance, security, and upkeep.

• **Risk of Second Move** – If the chosen retirement residence doesn't turn out to be a good fit, moving again could be disruptive.

Downsizing and Selling Your Home: Who Can I Ask for Help?

Philosophia
WITHIN

BUDGET FRIENDLY & COMMUNITY SUPPORT

Service	Who Can Help?	Average Cost	Pros	Cons
Realtor Services/ Repair & Upgrade Recommendations	Family friend in real estate, community real estate workshops	Free consultation, commission-based (2-7% of sale price)	Familiarity with your needs, potential reduced fees	May not have full expertise or marketing reach
Home Staging & Organization	Church groups, community volunteers, family, friends	Free or cost of materials	Personalized help, cost savings	May lack professional touch
Junk Removal & Decluttering	Local volunteer groups, Buy Nothing groups, charitable donation pickups	Free to small donation	Sustainable, community support	May require multiple pickups or trips
Home Cleaning	Family, friends, church members, neighborhood helpers	Free to small fee	Trustworthy, cost-effective	May not be as thorough as professionals, less private
Property Management	Trusted family member, neighbor	Free to small fee	Familiar person looking after property	Can be a burden on family or friends
Legal Help (Wills, Power of Attorney, Contracts)	Pro bono legal clinics, legal aid, community workshops	Free or reduced fee	Affordable, guidance available	Limited availability, may not cover complex needs
Packing & Moving Assistance	Friends, family, church youth groups, local volunteers	Free or cost of truck rental ($50–$200)	Supportive, cost-effective	Coordination needed, may take longer

Downsizing and Selling Your Home: Who Can I Hire to Help?

Philosophia
— WITHIN —

PROFESSIONAL & TURNKEY SERVICES

Service	Who Provides It?	Average Cost	Pros	Cons
Realtor Services/ Repair & Upgrade Recommendations	Professional real estate agents	Free consultation, commission-based (2-7% of sale price)	Market expertise, handles negotiations	Higher cost than DIY sale
Home Staging & Organization	Professional home stagers	$500–$3,000	Potential for increased home value, quick sale	Up-front cost
Junk Removal & Decluttering	Junk removal companies (1-800-GOT-JUNK, local haulers)	$100–$800 per load	Quick, efficient	Can be expensive
Home Cleaning	Cleaning companies (Molly Maid, local services)	$25–$300 per visit	Thorough, reliable	Recurring costs if ongoing
Property Management	Property management companies	$100–$300/ month	Handles maintenance, tenants	Ongoing cost
Legal Help (Wills, Power of Attorney, Contracts)	Elder law attorneys, estate planners	$200–$500/hour	Legal expertise, peace of mind	Expensive for complex cases
Packing & Moving Assistance	Moving companies (U-Haul, Two Men and a Truck)	$1,000–$5,000 (local move)	Less physical strain, quick move	Costly, may need coordination

Common Living Options for Older Adults

Option	Pros	Cons	Considerations	Next Steps
Successful Aging at Home	• Remain in familiar surroundings. • No moving stress or expenses. • Maintain independence and routines. • Possible home modifications for safety. • Can bring in private services if affordable.	• High maintenance costs (repairs, yard work, etc.). • Potential safety hazards (stairs, bathroom access, etc.). • Risk of isolation if transportation and social connections are limited. • Future health needs may require a sudden move. • Limited access to emergency or medical care.	• Can I afford home modifications (grab bars, ramps, stair lifts)? • Do I have a support network for errands, socialization, and emergencies? • Can I afford in-home care if needed in the future? • Do I have a plan for transportation if I stop driving? • Can I continue caring for my pet, and do I have a plan if I can't? • What are my current monthly expenses? • Do I qualify for financial assistance? • How much will home modifications and potential care cost? • Do I have savings or assets to cover future needs?	• Research modifications and costs • Connect with community support services • Create an emergency plan • Assess financial ability to hire private care • Apply for financial assistance if eligible ✓ Ensure legal affairs are in order—will, personal directive and power of attorney ✓ Stay proactive about health and mobility to maintain ✓ independence as long as possible.

Option	Pros	Cons	Considerations	Next Steps
Selling & Moving to a Senior Retirement Facility (i.e., Independent, Assisted, or Full Care)	• Various levels of care available based on needs. • Social opportunities and activities. • Meals, housekeeping, and medical care available. • Safety features and emergency response services. • No home maintenance responsibilities. • When needs increase you will ready and services will be available.	• Can be expensive (depending on services and location). • May have long waitlists (up to 2+ years for spots) • Less privacy compared to a private home. • Potential adjustment period to communal living and new area • Many facilities do not allow pets.	• What level of care do I need now and in the near future? • What is my budget? Do I qualify for low-income housing? • Have I applied for waitlists to secure a future spot? • Is the facility close to my support system? • Does the facility align with my social and lifestyle preferences? • Do they allow pets, and if not, do I have a rehoming plan? • If moving, what are the costs involved (real • estate fees, moving costs, deposits, etc.)? • Do I have savings or assets to cover future needs?	• Visit different facilities. • Apply for waitlists (subsidized and private). • Talk to residents and staff. • Review financial plans. • Apply for financial assistance if eligible. • Consult a financial planner or elder care advisor for budgeting assistance. ✓ Ensure legal affairs are in order—will, personal directive and power of attorney ✓ Stay proactive about health and mobility to maintain independence as long as possible.

Option	Pros	Cons	Considerations	Next Steps
Selling & Moving to a Smaller Home (Condo, Apartment, etc.)	• Less maintenance and lower costs than a house. • Possible access to amenities (fitness centers, social areas). • Can still hire private care services if needed. • More independence than a senior facility. • Some allow pets.	• No built-in care services (unless hired separately). • Potential for isolation if transportation and social access are limited. • Some condo fees or rental costs may be high. • May need to move again if health declines.	• Does this home meet my mobility and accessibility needs? • Can I afford additional in-home care if required? • Are there social and community activities nearby? • Will this move make me feel safer and more comfortable? • How close am I to medical facilities and my support system? • Does the building allow pets, and if not, do I have a rehoming plan? • If moving, what are the costs involved? • Do I have savings or assets to cover future needs?	• Research affordable condos and apartments. • Plan for moving costs. • Arrange transportation options. • Apply for financial assistance if eligible. • Consult a financial planner or elder care advisor for budgeting assistance. ✓ Ensure legal affairs are in order—will, personal directive and power of attorney ✓ Stay proactive about health and mobility to maintain independence as long as possible.

Option	Pros	Cons	Considerations	Next Steps
Moving in with a Family Member	• Provides emotional and social support. • Lower living expenses. • Easier access to family assistance when needed. • Shared responsibilities (meals, household chores, etc.).	• Potential loss of independence. • Adjusting to a different household dynamic. • Possible strain on family relationships. • Home may not be equipped for mobility or medical needs. • Less privacy. • Higher potential for elder abuse.	• Have I discussed expectations with my family? • Does the home accommodate my mobility and safety needs? • Will I have personal space and privacy? • What financial contributions will I be expected to make? • Is there a longterm plan if my care needs increase? • How will transportation, healthcare, and social activities be managed? • If I have a pet, is my family comfortable with it?	• Have a detailed conversation with family members. • Outline household expectations and responsibilities. • Ensure home modifications for accessibility if needed. • Discuss financial arrangements. • Plan for future care needs and independence. • Consult a financial planner or elder care advisor for budgeting assistance.

Option	Pros	Cons	Considerations	Next Steps
Home Sharing Home sharing can be defined as an arrangement between two or more people who share a dwelling. In the context of senior housing, home sharing is commonly undertaken by seniors who have a spare room in their home and offer reduced rent in exchange for chores and companionship.	• Provides emotional and social support. • Lower living expenses • Easier access to assistance when needed. • Shared responsibilities (meals, household chores, etc.).	• Potential loss of independence. • Adjusting to a different household dynamic. • Possible strain on family relationships. • Home may not be equipped for mobility or medical needs. • Less privacy. • Higher potential for elder abuse.	• Have I discussed expectations with my a potential roommate? • Does the home accommodate my mobility and safety needs? • Will I have personal space and privacy? • What financial plans need to be made? • Is there a longterm plan if my care needs increase? • How will transportation, healthcare, and social activities be managed? • Will I be comfortable with a roommate bringing a pet?	• Have a detailed conversation with family members. • Outline household expectations and responsibilities. • Ensure home modifications for accessibility if needed. • Discuss financial arrangements. • Plan for future care needs and independence. • Consult a financial planner or elder care advisor for budgeting assistance.

Comparison of Common Senior Housing Options

*Info subject to change and varies by region - Refer to resources at the back of this book.

Option	Best For/Features	Care Level	Costs & Funding	Challenges
Independent Living (IL) / Retirement Communities	Active seniors who can live independently but prefer a community setting. **Features:** • Private apartments or homes • communal dining • housekeeping • social activities • security	**Minimal** (some services available, but no medical care).	$1,500–$6,000/month (varies by location and services; mostly private pay).	✕ High cost (not covered by government programs). ✕ No medical support (seniors may need to relocate if care needs increase). ✕ Social adjustment (moving away from familiar surroundings can be difficult).
Assisted Living (AL)	Seniors needing help with daily activities (bathing, dressing, medication management). **Features:** • Private/semiprivate units • dining services • housekeeping • personal care • 24/7 staff	**Moderate** (some nursing assistance, but not full-time medical care).	$2,000–$6,500/month (some government subsidies available).	✕ Expensive (especially for private-pay residents). ✕ Limited medical care (not suitable for those needing intensive nursing). ✕ Varied regulations (quality and services can differ by state/province).

Option	Best For/Features	Care Level	Costs & Funding	Challenges
Supportive Living	Seniors needing moderate-to-high support but not fulltime medical care. **Features:** • Personal care • nursing support • medication management • meals • housekeeping	**Moderate to high**	$1,500–$4,000/month (government subsidies may apply).	✕ Limited availability (varies by province and funding). ✕ Not fully covered by government (seniors may still need private funds). ✕ May require relocation if medical needs increase.
Long-Term Care (LTC) / Nursing Homes	Seniors with chronic illnesses requiring 24/7 nursing care. **Features:** • Medical care • rehabilitation • social programs • meals • housekeeping	**High** (licensed nurses and medical staff).	$1,500–$3,500/month (government subsidies available).	✕ Long waitlists (especially for government funded beds). ✕ Institutional feel (less privacy, shared rooms common). ✕ Limited personal freedom (scheduled meals, structured routines).
Memory Care / Secure Dementia Care	Seniors with Alzheimer's or dementia requiring specialized care. **Features:** • 24/7 security • structured routines • cognitive therapies • specialized staff	**High**	$3,500–$8,000/month (some subsidies available).	✕ Very expensive (especially private facilities). ✕ Emotional distress (transitioning can be difficult for both seniors and families). ✕ Limited availability (demand often exceeds supply).

Option	Best For/Features	Care Level	Costs & Funding	Challenges
Senior Lodges	Low-income seniors needing affordable housing with some support. **Features:** • Basic accommodations • meal services • housekeeping • social activities	**Low**	$1,000–$3,000/ month (subsidized options available).	✕ Basic amenities (few luxury services or medical support). ✕ Long waitlists (especially for government-funded spots). ✕ Limited care options (may require relocation as needs increase).
Continuing Care Retirement Communities (CCRCs) / Life Plan Communities	Seniors wanting a long-term care plan in one community. **Features:** • Includes independent living, assisted living, and nursing care in one location.	**Varies** (adjusts as needs change).	$2,500–6,000/ month (limited availability).	✕ Very costly (upfront buy-in plus monthly fees). ✕ Not widely available (more common in the US than Canada). ✕ Financial risk (if the community shuts down or funds run out).
Home Care / Successful Aging at Home	Seniors who prefer to stay at home but need assistance. **Features:** Personal supports for a fee such as: • lawn care • snow removal • housekeeping • nursing care • meal delivery • companionship	**Varies** (from light assistance to full-time inhome nursing).	$25–$50/ hour (limited government funded home care available).	✕ High cost for full-time care (24/7 in-home nursing is very expensive). ✕ Home modifications required (ramps, grab bars, stair lifts may be needed). ✕ Caregiver burnout (family members often provide unpaid support).

Funding Resources for Senior Facilities

*Info subject to change and varies by region - Refer to resources at the back of this book.

Funding Type	Funding Source	Funding Type and Examples
Government-Funded Long-Term Care (LTC) & Home Care	**Provincial Health Ministries** Each province provides subsidized long-term care and home care services. Check with your state, province or territory)	**Examples:** **Ontario**: Long-Term Care Home Funding (OHIP covers basic costs, residents pay a co-pay). **Alberta**: Designated Supportive Living & LTC (Alberta Health Services covers medical care, residents pay accommodation fees). **British Columbia**: Home and Community Care (subsidized home care and assisted living options).
Guaranteed Income Supplement (GIS)	**Federal Government** For low-income seniors receiving Old Age Security (OAS).	Helps cover housing and care costs.
Veterans Affairs Canada (VAC) Benefits	**Federal Government**	**Veterans Independence Program (VIP):** Helps eligible veterans pay for home care, assisted living, and LTC. **Long-Term Care Program:** Provides full or partial funding for LTC homes for veterans.

Funding Type	Funding Source	Funding Type and Examples
Provincial/State Seniors' Benefits	**Provincial Health Ministries, varies by province, state or territory.**	**Alberta**: Alberta Seniors Benefit (ASB) Helps low income seniors pay for accommodations, personal supports, medical supplies, extended health benefits, etc. **British Columbia**: BC Seniors' Supplement – Additional financial assistance for lowincome seniors. **Quebec**: Shelter Allowance Program – Helps seniors with rent and living costs.
Nonprofit & Subsidized Housing for Seniors	**Provincial Government** Many provinces have low-income senior housing options such as lodges and supportive housing.	**Example**: Alberta's Seniors Lodge Program (affordable housing on a sliding scale according to income, with meals and housekeeping).
Investments / Employer Pensions	**Registered Retirement Savings Plan (RRSP) & Registered Retirement Income Fund (RRIF)**	Seniors can withdraw funds from RRSPs or RRIFs to pay for care.

Aging at Home: Services, Costs and Funding

*Info subject to change and varies by region - Refer to resources at the back of this book.

Service	Potential Costs & Funding Options (CAD)	Creative Alternatives
Personal Care & Home Support Services Assistance with bathing, dressing, grooming, toileting, and mobility.	**Cost**: $25–$50/hour **Monthly Estimate**: $1,500–$4,000 (20–40 hrs./week) **Funding & Subsidies:** Provincial Home Care Programs (e.g., Ontario's Home and Community Care)	Some communities have care cooperatives where seniors pool resources to hire shared caregivers.
Housekeeping & Laundry Services Cleaning, laundry, dishwashing, and light maintenance.	**Cost**: $50–$200 per visit (2-person crew/1-4 hrs.) **Monthly Estimate**: $50–$800 (1–4 visits/month) **Funding & Subsidies:** Veterans Affairs Canada (VAC) – Housekeeping Assistance	"Senior-for-senior" home services, where retired individuals offer affordable assistance to other seniors.
Meal Delivery & Nutrition Services Healthy, prepared meals delivered to the home or personal grocery shopping.	**Cost:** **Meal delivery**: $8–$15 per meal (e.g., Heart to Home Meals, Meals on Wheels) **Personal grocery shopping**: $25–$50/hour **Grocery Delivery Services**: (e.g., Instacart, Voila, Uber) $8-$20 per delivery + grocery costs **Monthly Estimate**: $250–$1,500 **Funding & Subsidies:** Meals on Wheels (subsidized meal delivery for seniors)	Subscription-based meal prep services customized by nutritionists for dietary needs (e.g., Chefs Plate, Hello Fresh)

Service	Potential Costs & Funding Options (CAD)	Creative Alternatives
Transportation Services Rides to medical appointments, grocery stores, or social events.	**Cost:** **Private driver**: $25–$60/hour **Volunteer Senior ride services**: $5–$20 per trip (e.g., Drive Happiness, Friendly Volunteer Driver programs) **Monthly Estimate**: $200–$800 **Funding & Subsidies:** Local senior transportation grants (varies by province)	Volunteer "buddy drivers"— younger seniors provide rides to older seniors in exchange for credits they can use later.
Home Healthcare & Nursing Injections, wound care, medication administration, chronic disease management.	**Cost**: $50–$120/hour **Monthly Estimate**: $2,000–$7,000 (varies by needs) **Funding & Subsidies:** Provincial home nursing programs (e.g., Alberta Health Services Home Care)	Hybrid care models combining telehealth, virtual and, in-home nurse visits to reduce costs.
Respite Care for Family Caregivers Temporary relief for primary caregivers.	**Cost**: $25–$50/hour or $150–$300 per overnight stay **Monthly Estimate**: $500–$3,000 **Funding & Subsidies:** Caregiver Benefit Programs (e.g., Ontario's Family Caregiver Leave)	Subscription-based meal prep services customized by nutritionists for dietary needs. (e.g., Chefs Plate, Hello Fresh)
Adult Day Programs Enriching activities in a structured program.	**Cost**: $0-$180/day **Funding & Subsidies:** Consult local heath authorities, VA, and government for subsidies and programs.	

Service	Potential Costs & Funding Options (CAD)	Creative Alternatives
Companion & Social Engagement Services Friendly visits, games, outings, and emotional support.	**Cost**: $30–$50/hour **Monthly Estimate**: $200–$2,000 **Funding & Subsidies:** Local community grants for senior companionship programs	Intergenerational roommate programs, where college students live with seniors at reduced rent in exchange for companionship.
Home Modifications & Safety Upgrades Grab bars, stair lifts, ramps, and fall prevention modifications.	**Cost:** **Minor modifications:** $200–$2,000 **Major renovations:** $5,000–$30,000 **Funding & Subsidies:** Home Accessibility Tax Credit (HATC), Seniors Home Adaptation and Repair (Loan) Program (SHARP), The Canada $5000 Senior Grant, Residential Access Modification Program (RAMP)	Community-based home modification co-ops, where groups of seniors invest in safety upgrades at discounted rates.
Smart Technology & Monitoring Services Fall detection, medication reminders, emergency alerts.	**Cost:** **Medical alert system:** $20–$100/month **Smart home automation:** $500–$5,000 (one-time installation) **Funding & Subsidies:** Assistive Devices Program (ADP) for medical alert systems	Voice-activated AI companions providing safety checks and reminders
Financial Support for Family Caregivers Programs that pay family members to provide Care	**Canada Caregiver Credit (CCC)**: Tax relief for caregivers, **Compassionate Care Benefits** (EI Program), **Paid leave for caregivers**. **Provincial Caregiver Allowances**: Alberta, Nova Scotia, and Quebec offer financial aid.	

Let's Consider Special Situations

While many factors influence our ability to live and age well, some individuals face unique circumstances that deserve special attention. Let's explore these with compassion and understanding—together.

"I honor the unique journey of every soul, including my own. With compassion and understanding, I embrace the wisdom and beauty in our differences, knowing we all deserve to live and age well."

– My Soul

Aging with Pride: Understanding the Needs of Older 2SLGBTQIA+ Adults

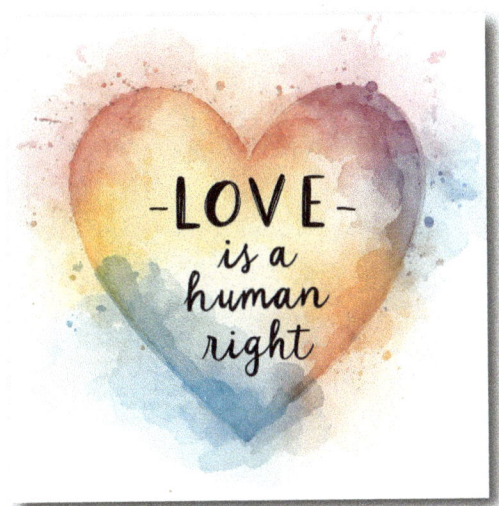

As societal attitudes toward the 2SLGBTQIA+ community evolve, the experiences of older 2SLGBTQIA+ adults provide a crucial perspective on both the progress made and the challenges that remain. Steven Krahn, a retirement living consultant, offers insight into the unique struggles and triumphs of aging as an 2SLGBTQIA+ individual.

Steven Krahn, BEd, is a retired teacher who taught grades one through nine in St. Albert. After retiring from teaching, he became a program facilitator for an Edmonton-based seniors service provider, where he supported seniors living with dementia through recreational programming. Today, Steven serves as a retirement living consultant—a role that includes responsibilities as a leasing manager, business development manager, and community support liaison. He also brings his deep knowledge and skill set to support the Edmonton Seniors Pride Group in their efforts to build an 2SLGBTQIA+ retirement home in Edmonton.

The Shifting Landscape of Acceptance

Steven recalls growing up in rural Alberta, where being openly gay was not only stigmatized but dangerous. "It was common for people to 'hunt faggots,' and coming out in small-town Alberta was life-threatening," he sadly shares. While society has progressed, there is still work to be done. Today, physical violence is less tolerated, but discrimination persists in more subtle ways, particularly in senior living communities.

Unique Challenges in Aging and Healthcare

Many older 2SLGBTQIA+ adults face difficulties in securing inclusive retirement or assisted living arrangements. "Some are forced to go back into the closet to fit in," Steven explains. Additionally, financial instability remains a concern, as historical discrimination prevented many from securing well-paying, pensionable careers. While Steven himself has not experienced healthcare bias since coming out in 2021, he acknowledges that many older 2SLGBTQIA+ individuals still encounter prejudice in medical and care settings. In fact, many have remained hesitant or even fearful of being open about their identities with healthcare professionals, due to past experiences of discrimination or outright hostility. This fear often results in inadequate care or avoidance of critical services, further isolating individuals who are already vulnerable.

Building Inclusive Communities

While progress is evident, assisted living and senior care facilities still need to enhance inclusivity. "Education is key," Steven emphasizes, noting that younger generations are more accepting, but many older residents require awareness training. "Once given, education fosters change," he adds. However, deeply rooted religious biases still create barriers in some communities.

The Importance of Chosen Family

For Steven, coming out meant losing extended family ties due to religious intolerance. "My children have been wonderful, and I've built a network of affirming friendships," he says. Chosen families play a vital role for many 2SLGBTQIA+ seniors who face isolation and rejection from biological relatives.

Wellness and Self-Care

Steven stresses the importance of authenticity in well-being. "I tried to hide in plain sight for years, but it took a toll on my mental health. After coming out, I became healthier—mentally, physically, and spiritually." He also practices mindfulness, stays active, and continuously challenges himself to grow.

Advice for Future Generations

"Live your full self," Steven advises younger 2SLGBTQIA+ individuals. "Don't let society dictate who you should be. Stay fit—mentally, physically, and spiritually." He also encourages seeking joy, embracing adventure, and fostering resilience despite hardships.

A Call for Respect in Care

For healthcare professionals, caregivers, and families, Steven's message is clear: "Respect goes a long way. Respect gender identity, relationships, and individual expressions. Don't expect people to change to fit societal molds—broaden the rules and expectations."

As we strive to create more inclusive spaces, the voices of older 2SLGBTQIA+ adults like Steven offer invaluable guidance on how to foster dignity, respect, and support in aging communities.

Aging with Pride: A Vision Realized

Building on the voices and experiences of advocates like Steven Krahn, we turn now to the remarkable story of a groundbreaking project in Edmonton, Alberta—one that has been over a decade in the making and is rooted in the powerful belief that older 2SLGBTQIA+ adults deserve to live and age with dignity, safety, respect, and the freedom to be their authentic selves.

EDMONTON PRIDE SENIORS GROUP

Creating Inclusive Spaces For 2SLGBTQIA+ Older Adults

Michael Phair, a well-known Edmonton advocate and community leader, currently coordinates the Edmonton Pride Seniors Group. His advocacy spans decades, including his work as a city councillor from 1992–2007, founding member of the AIDS Network of Edmonton (now HIV Edmonton), and long-time voice for equity in education, housing, and healthcare. With the Edmonton Pride Seniors Group, Michael has helped realize a long- held dream: **the development of Alberta's first 2SLGBTQIA+-affirming retirement residence.**

Over thirteen years ago, the initiative began informally when a small group of four to five older 2SLGBTQIA+ adults began to ask a vital question: What resources exist for aging individuals in their community? The answer, they discovered, was very little. Partnering with SAGE Seniors Association and later supported by municipal grants, the group expanded to ten to fifteen regular participants and initiated formal rolling surveys to better understand the needs and hopes of 2SLGBTQIA+ older adults across the Edmonton region.

Many of the survey responses were striking—not just in what was said, but in what had never before been voiced. Michael explained that many of the respondents shared they had never considered aging because "they didn't expect to live that long." The trauma of the AIDS crisis, paired with lifelong discrimination, left many believing they would not reach their sixties, seventies, or beyond. But with the help of modern medicine and increased societal awareness, many have outlived those fears—only to find themselves aging with little family support, financial stability, or safe, affirming housing.

Another challenge that emerged was a widespread hesitation—often deep-seated fear—among 2SLGBTQIA+ seniors about revealing their identity to healthcare professionals. Many older adults have endured decades of being pathologized, dismissed, or openly discriminated against by medical providers. Even today, this fear leads many to conceal their identity, resulting in barriers to accessing appropriate and compassionate care, and sometimes forego vital health services altogether.

In response to these findings, the Edmonton Pride Seniors Group hosted a small symposium and invited international advocates to share strategies for inclusive senior care. They collaborated with universities, mainstream senior housing organizations, and community stakeholders to develop a comprehensive prospectus of what affirming aging could look like for 2SLGBTQIA+ older adults.

Now, after years of perseverance, collaboration, and determination, their vision is becoming a reality. In partnership with Right at Home Housing Society (RAHH)—a respected nonprofit leader in providing affordable housing for marginalized communities—the group has secured land in east Edmonton (at 95 Street/101A Avenue & Rowland Road) to construct a seventy-to eighty-unit independent living facility. With accessible transportation, parking, and a variety of suite sizes to accommodate different incomes, this development is a shining example of what it means to age with pride with community.

As of 2025, the project is being re-costed due to the economic impacts of the COVID-19 pandemic and ongoing trade tariffs by the USA. Despite these challenges, the team remains hopeful and focused, with plans to launch a capital campaign in 2025/2026 to bring the project to completion by the summer of 2026.

This milestone is more than a building—it is a beacon of hope. It represents years of grassroots advocacy, lived experience, and an unyielding commitment to equity in aging for all. As Michael and his colleagues have shown, lasting change comes not only from speaking out but from building up—from creating spaces where people can live out their final decades with authenticity, companionship, and care.

To learn more or support this project, **visit www.epsg.ca**. Your awareness, compassion, and contributions can help make this long-overdue dream a sustainable reality.

Special Considerations for Rural Older Adults

Living on Acreages, Farms, or in Remote Areas

As health needs change, older adults living in rural areas, on farms, or on acreages face unique challenges when deciding whether to age in place or transition to a new living situation. **Here are key factors to consider:**

Home & Property Maintenance

Is the home and land manageable as mobility and strength decline? Are there reliable services for snow removal, lawn care, home repairs, and general upkeep? Are there modifications needed for safety (ramps, railings, accessible bathrooms, etc.)?

Accessibility & Transportation

How far is the nearest grocery store, pharmacy, or medical facility? Is there access to reliable transportation if driving is no longer an option? Are roads well-maintained year-round (especially in winter)?

Emergency Services & Healthcare Access

How quickly can emergency responders reach the home? Are there local home care or nursing services available? Are telehealth or virtual healthcare services accessible with good internet connectivity? How far is the nearest hospital or specialist care?

Isolation & Social Connection

Are friends, family, or community services nearby for social support? Are there community programs for seniors, such as meal delivery, check-in services, or senior centers? Is there reliable internet access for virtual connections and entertainment?

Farming & Livestock Responsibilities

Is there a plan for farm operations if physically unable to manage them? Is there someone available to help with daily tasks such as feeding animals or managing crops? Are there financial or legal plans in place for farm succession or land transfer?

Safety & Security

Is there a security plan for living alone (medical alert system, monitored alarms, check-in calls) Is the property well-lit and safe to navigate at night? Are there backup power sources in case of outages (especially for medical equipment)?

WWW.PHILOSOPHIAWITHIN.COM

Care Considerations for Pet Owners

 This one can be tough. Let's talk it through.

As health needs change, older adults with pets must consider how to best care for their furry companions while ensuring their own well-being.

Whether aging at home or considering a move, here are key factors to consider:

Daily Pet Care Responsibilities

Can you safely provide daily care, including feeding, grooming, and exercise? Are there mobility limitations that make tasks like bending, lifting, or walking difficult? Is there a support system in place (family, friends, or pet services) to assist when needed?

Housing & Pet Policies

If moving, does the new home or facility allow pets? Are there size, breed, or species restrictions? Are there pet-friendly housing options nearby?

Veterinary Care & Health Needs

Is there a veterinarian nearby, and can you access appointments easily? Does the pet require frequent medical care or special dietary needs? Are pet expenses manageable within your budget?

Pet Insurance

Pet insurance helps cover unexpected vet bills from accidents or illnesses, and some plans even include routine checkups and wellness care. The cost depends on your pet's age, breed, and where you live. Most policies have an annual deductible and then reimburse you for a percentage of the covered expenses. It may be helpful to investigate the common health concerns of a particular animal prior to adding a new family pet.

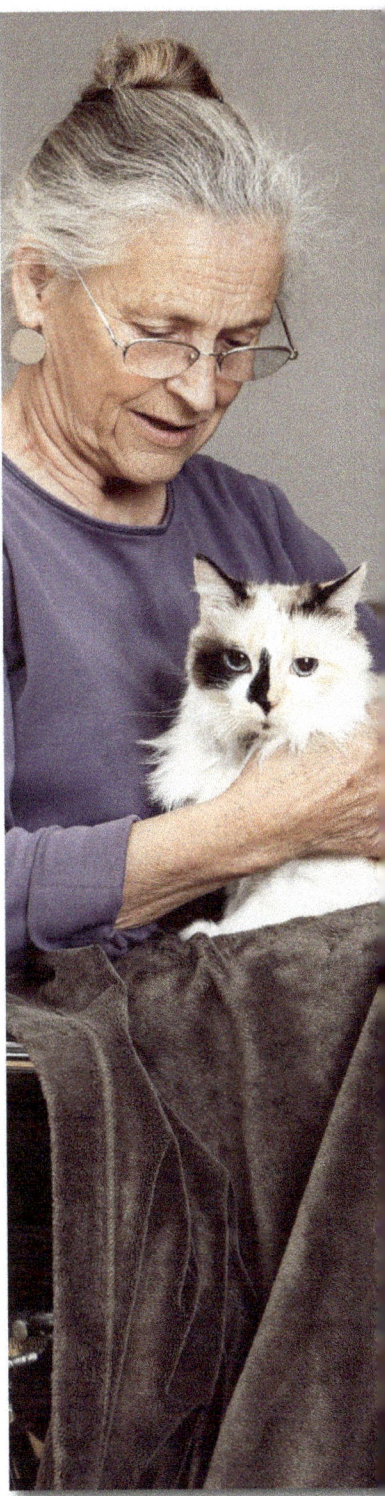

Assistance & Support Services

Are there local pet-sitting or dog-walking services available? Are there programs that assist seniors with pet care (e.g., veterinary assistance programs, etc.)? Is there a backup caregiver in case of illness or hospitalization?

Exercise & Mobility

If the pet requires walks, is there a safe way to provide exercise? Are there nearby green spaces or pet-friendly areas? Are alternative solutions available, such as hiring a dog walker or using an enclosed yard?

Emotional Well-Being & Companionship

How important is your pet to your mental and emotional health? Would rehoming or separation cause distress, and what are alternative solutions? Are there therapy pet programs if keeping a pet becomes too difficult?

Planning for the Future

Have you designated a trusted person to care for your pet in case of emergency or long-term illness? Is there a written pet care plan or pet trust in place? If rehoming becomes necessary, are there family, friends, or rescue organizations that can help?

WWW.PHILOSOPHIAWITHIN.COM

Cultural & Indigenous Considerations

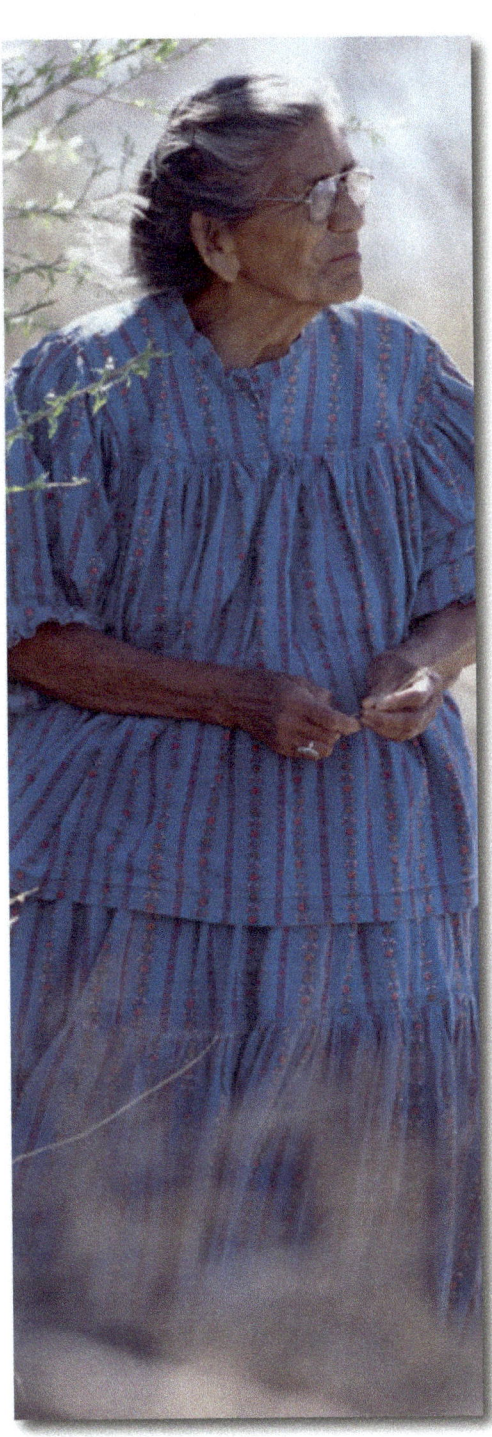

Older adults from diverse cultural and Indigenous backgrounds in Canada & the US face unique challenges and opportunities when planning for aging and long-term care. Recognizing these factors ensures respectful and inclusive decision-making.

Cultural Considerations

- **Multigenerational Living** – Preference for aging at home with family over senior facilities.
- **Language & Communication** – Access to services in the senior's first language.
- **Culturally Specific Housing** – Residences tailored to traditions and languages.
- **Dietary Needs** – Religious/cultural dietary accommodations (e.g., kosher, halal).
- **Religious & Spiritual Practices** – Access to worship and faith-based activities.
- **Healthcare Beliefs** – Preference for traditional or holistic medicine alongside conventional care.
- **End-of-Life Customs** – Respect for cultural funeral and burial traditions.

Indigenous Considerations

- **Aging in Community** – Elders prefer staying in familiar surroundings.
- **Respect for Elders** – Their wisdom and role in decision-making should be honored.
- **Traditional Healing** – Access to ceremonies, smudging and Indigenous medicine.
- **Rural & Remote Challenges** – Limited access to healthcare and services.

- **Mobility & Transportation** – Distance to medical care and family impacts choices.
- **Elder Abuse Risks** – Financial exploitation and coercion concerns.
- **Trauma-Informed Support** – Addressing residential school and systemic injustices.
- **Housing Shortages** – Overcrowding and lack of Indigenous-specific elder housing.
- **Connection to Land** – Desire to remain on traditional lands.

Challenges for Older Adults:

✓ Limited culturally inclusive senior housing
✓ Rural and systemic barriers to healthcare
✓ Cultural isolation in mainstream facilities

> *Informed choices ensure older adults can age with dignity, respect and cultural connection.*

Opportunities for Older Adult Care Providers:

✓ Growth of culturally tailored housing and services
✓ Expansion of Indigenous-led senior programs
✓ Greater recognition of traditional healing

Wisdom in Design

An Interview with Indigenous Architect Jim Gladue

"I'm most proud of fulfilling the dreams of my late parents, where my Dad wanted me to be an artist and my late, dear Mother wanted me to do architectural design. It was my parents who made me believe anything is possible."

When Jim Gladue, now age fifty-eight, reflects on his journey, he sees a life shaped by land, family, resilience, and culture. Born on Kehewin Cree Nation and raised in Edmonton by his strong, single mother—who raised eleven children and survived the legacy of residential schools—Jim's early life was grounded in survival, sacrifice, and an unwavering belief in the value of education.

"My mom always asked us, 'What are you going be when you grow up?' She pushed us to pursue higher education in our individual areas of interest and talent, and she believed in each of us. That foundation has stayed with me and my brothers and sisters."

Although he didn't graduate high school at first, Jim returned to learning with determination. He studied at Concordia, earned an architectural technology diploma from NAIT, and went on to study Native studies, as well as, art and design, at the University of Alberta. In his forties, he added IT animation and web design to his skill set.

At thirty-eight, he founded Gladue Designs, an innovative firm where art, architecture, Indigenous culture, and community planning come together.

Rooted in Culture, Growing Through Design

Jim's designs aren't just buildings—they are living embodiments of Cree values and teachings. His architectural expressions are infused with cultural symbolism, from the structure of a tipi to the circular form of a sweat lodge.

"There's no formal map for Cree architecture—it's guided by symbolism, tradition, and practicality. A tipi uses the straightest trees, placed in a sixteen-sided pattern. It's strong, functional, and meaningful. But I also consider accessibility. A sweat lodge is a traditional dome, yes—but for Elders with mobility challenges, it's not always usable. That's where design has to meet culture and care."

Jim draws deeply on the teachings of his parents, whom he considers the most influential Elders in his life.

"My father handed me a piece of wood and some old paint when I was sixteen. I had never painted before. He told me to paint it. What came out surprised us both—it was beautiful. That moment awakened something in me. My parents made me believe anything is possible."

Indigenous Perspectives on Aging

In Cree communities, aging isn't merely about reaching a certain age—it's about embodying wisdom and being chosen by the community as an Elder.

"Elders earn their place through knowledge and respect. It's not automatic. Elders are the carriers of stories, teachings, and values. But too often, there are limited spaces for them to share that wisdom."

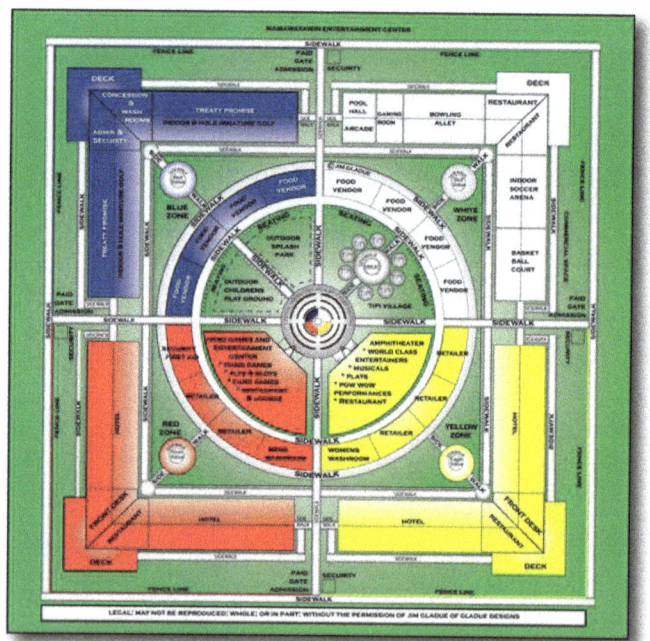

This realization drives Jim to design venues that honor and include Elders—spaces that are physically accessible, culturally relevant, and spiritually welcoming.

He defines aging well as a holistic journey—living in balance mentally, physically, spiritually, and emotionally.

"It's about learning and growing, even as you age. My farming project, for example, reflects that. Like the story of the Three Little Pigs. Life is like a wolf—are you building a house of straw, wood, or brick? I want to care for and expand what I've been given and build a sustainable life—and help others to do the same."

Innovative Projects: Healing the Land, Honoring the People

Jim's work spans a wide range of community-centered projects:

Kistikew Farming Project

Located on family land once used by his musham (grandfather), Jim's vision is to revive Indigenous farming traditions—supporting cattle, crops, and gardens that feed both body and spirit and provide for his community.

"My parents were farmers. The land has always given to us. This project is about food sovereignty, sustainability, and healing. What's good for this land is good for our people."

Kehewin Cree Nation Community Centre

By repurposing an old school into a vibrant community hub, Jim designed a space for employment, creativity, culture, and connection across generations.

"It's not just about reusing a building—it's about reigniting community spirit through art, food, sport, and shared stories."

Mamawayawin Entertainment Centre

Meaning "gathering place," this visionary cultural venue is shaped like the medicine wheel and integrates sacred Cree animals, cardinal directions, and color symbolism.

"This is a place for teaching, celebration, and healing. We're telling our story through design. It's a design to inspire pride and economic growth."

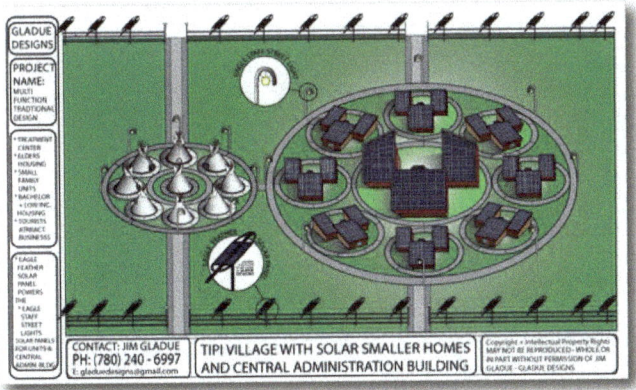

Designing with Dignity: Honoring Elders in Space

From Tipi Tiny Homes shaped like an eagle in flight to elder housing that maximizes light, warmth, and beauty, Jim's work consistently centers culture, dignity, independence, and community.

"Each Elder home faces south to maximize solar heating. The eagle design and art structures represent protection and vision. I asked the Creator and the eagle spirit for guidance in that design."

Healing Grounds: Reclaiming and Reconnecting

At the Devon Healing Medicine Grounds, Jim contributed his technical expertise to turning an old baseball field into a sacred site of education and ceremony.

"It's open to the public to learn about Indigenous medicine, the four directions, the sacred teachings. It was supported by the Town of Devon, and it's on Treaty 6 land. That acknowledgment is powerful and I am proud to have been part of it."

Building Forward: A Legacy of Possibility

Looking ahead, Jim hopes to expand the presence of Indigenous-led design in housing, health, and healing.

"I want to see Cree architecture become known and recognizable. I want to show that my mother was right—that anything is possible. That being proud of your culture can be shown in the buildings we live, heal, and grow in."

His legacy is not just physical structures but an invitation to listen, learn, and live with respect—for land, for tradition, and for one another, while being open to new ideas to meet modern needs.

"Work hard. Stay rooted in your culture. And listen to the people who love you. Not the ones who tear you down for lack of vision or understanding."

Inspired by Jim Gladue's vision?

To explore his work, support his projects, or bring Indigenous wisdom and design into your own space, visit: gladuedesigns. wixsite.com/gladued esigns

Contact Jim directly through his site to learn more or collaborate.

Hospital Discharge Checklist for Returning Home

This checklist helps ensure a safe and smooth transition from hospital to home. Use it to identify key considerations and support services needed.

☀ Immediate Safety Considerations

- Home Safety Assessment (Check for fall hazards, clutter, loose rugs, etc.)
- Mobility Aids (Walker, cane, wheelchair, grab bars, stair lift, etc.)
- Medication Management (Proper storage, dosage schedule, potential side effects)
- Emergency Plan (Medical alert system, emergency contacts posted, phone within reach)
- Accessibility (Bedroom, bathroom, and kitchen accessibility; temporary modifications if needed)
- Proper Nutrition & Hydration (Easy meal access, meal delivery options if required)
- Personal Hygiene Support (Bathing, dressing, toileting assistance if needed)
- Pain Management (Prescription fulfillment, follow-up with doctor or pain specialist)
- Post-Hospital Monitoring (Check for new/worsening symptoms, infection, dehydration, etc.)
- Caregiver Support (Family, friend, or hired help available for assistance)

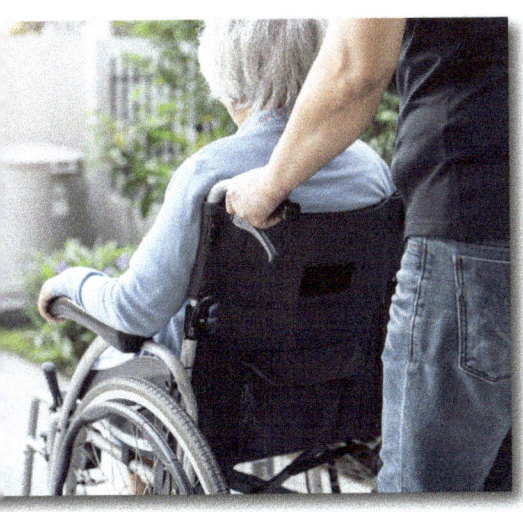

☀ Typical Discharge Services Arranged by the Hospital

- Discharge Plan & Follow-Up Instructions
- Referral to Home Care Services (if eligible)
- Equipment Loan (Walker, wheelchair, commode if needed)
- Prescription Review & Medication Reconciliation
- Transportation Arrangements (if required)
- Physiotherapy or Rehab Referrals
- Follow-Up Appointments with Specialists

☀ Services That Are Often Up to the Patient to Arrange

- Private Nursing or Personal Support Services
- Additional Home Modifications & Equipment
- Housekeeping, Meal Preparation, and Transportation
- Legal & Financial Planning for Long-Term Care
- Senior Companionship and Respite Care

Next Steps After Discharge

- Schedule follow-up medical appointments
- Arrange for required home support services
- Monitor recovery progress and adjust support as needed
- Discuss long-term care options if home is not a safe long-term solution

Not Ready to Move?

☀ Proactive Planning for a Future Move: Making the Process Easier

Even if you're not ready to move yet, taking small steps now can make future transitions smoother for you and your family, reduce stress, and give you more control over your decisions.

Start Preparing Early

- **Declutter & Organize Now** – Sorting through belongings over time prevents last-minute overwhelm.
- **Assess Your Current Home** – Identify what modifications might be needed to safely age in place.
- **Create a Moving Timeline** – Even if it's years away, having a rough plan can ease decision-making.

Ask for Help & Support

- **Involve Family & Friends** – Loved ones may be happy to help with sorting, packing, or emotional support.
- **Hire Professionals When Needed** – Consider professional organizers, estate planners, or senior move managers to help.
- **Join a Support Group** – Connecting with others going through similar transitions can be reassuring.

Budget-Friendly & Practical Downsizing

- **Tackle One Room at a Time** – Start with nonsentimental items like kitchen gadgets or paperwork.
- **Use a Combination Approach** – Mix DIY efforts with professional services where needed.
- **Sell or Donate Unused Items** – Estate sales, consignment shops, online selling, and charities can help repurpose belongings.

Maintain Control Over Your Future

- **Decide Where You Might Want to Live** – Explore housing options in advance, so you're not rushed later.
- **Research Moving & Storage Services** – Knowing your options ahead of time helps avoid last-minute scrambling.
- **Consider a Trial Stay** – Some senior communities allow short stays to experience life there before making a decision.
- **Acknowledge the Sentimental Aspect** – It's okay to feel emotional when letting go of items.
- **Take Photos of Important Items** – A digital memory can be just as meaningful.
- **Celebrate Small Wins** – Each step brings you closer to a smoother transition when the time comes.

Plan for the emotional side of making changes— this is often the toughest part! Do this well and the rest will fall into place. Take small steps at your own pace, knowing you're setting yourself up for a future that aligns with your needs and preferences.

WWW.PHILOSOPHIAWITHIN.COM

Let's Assess

Taking the time to thoughtfully and intentionally
review and reflect on each area of your life
will put you on the path to aging well.

*"Clarity comes with action. Once a decision is
made, the path forward reveals itself."*

– Unknown

Living and Aging Well
Readiness Statement

Philosophia
WITHIN

How to Use This Assessment

By working through each step of this **Living & Aging Well Readiness Assessment** you can assess your current situation, reflect on areas that may need improvement, explore living options, and create a personalized action plan for the future.

STEP 1: ASSESS YOUR READINESS TO LIVE AND AGE WELL IN KEY AREAS

This step includes a checklist to help you evaluate how prepared you are to remain in your home and community as you age. It covers nine key areas of your life:

1. My Health
2. My Home
3. My Transportation
4. My Finances
5. My Social Connections
6. My Safety
7. My Supports and Services
8. My Community
9. My Partner (and Me)

Each section contains a series of statements. For each one, mark "Yes" or "No" based on your current situation. If a statement does not apply to you, leave it blank. Once completed, your responses will give you a clearer picture of your preparedness for aging in place.

STEP 2: REFLECT ON YOUR NEEDS AND PRIORITIES

After completing the checklist, tally up your answers and take time to reflect on areas where you may need improvement. Use this section as a mini-planning guide to note what actions you want to take in each of the nine areas. You can refer back to this section periodically to track your progress and update your plans as needed.

Next, move on to Step 3: Creating Your Personal Action Plan with SMART goals.

☀ MY HEALTH

There are laws that allow people close to you to make healthcare decisions on your behalf if you can't make them yourself, such as a power of attorney, or naming someone to help you make healthcare decisions, as in a personal directive. Speak to a legal advocate to find out about making these essential documents.

Think about your state of health as it is now. What can you do now to help ensure a healthy future?

MY HEALTH	YES	NO
I am physically active and do a variety of physical activities that I enjoy.		
I eat several servings of fruit and vegetables in a day.		
I have a healthy body weight that has remained the same for the past six months.		
I schedule regular appointments for physical, vision, dental, and hearing checkups.		
I know what screening tests are recommended for my age and discuss these with my doctor.		
I avoid alcohol when taking medication, or check with a doctor or pharmacist first.		
I do not smoke, or I have a plan to quit in the future.		
If I drink alcohol, I stay below the limits suggested for adults my age.		

MY HEALTH	YES	NO
I generally experience good mental health. I am aware of the signs and symptoms of depression/anxiety, and if they continue, I will take steps to address them.		
I know how to keep my bones healthy and strong and have discussed this with my doctor or other healthcare professional.		
I have talked with my doctor about my preexisting medical condition and what services and supports I may need as I age.		
I keep my mind active daily through a variety of interests and hobbies and learning new things.		
I am aware of my family's medical history and have talked with my doctor about what I can do now to maintain my health and how my healthcare needs may change as I age.		
I am aware of electronic tools, such as medication reminders and health management systems that will allow me to remain healthy.		
I have written down and shared my wishes for care with my family in the event I become incapable of giving my consent.		
I participate in activities and/or consult with a variety of professionals, which address my health needs in a holistic way—body, mind, soul and spirit.		
I am proactive with my health and consult with alternative healthcare professionals as needed, such as chiropractors, naturopaths, others and others.		
TOTAL of all YES and NO answers:		

☀ MY HOME

Think about the home you live in now. Do you plan to live there when you are seventy or eighty years of age or older? Do you own or rent? If you rent, your ability to make changes to your home to support your needs may be limited.

Consider what you can do to age well at home as a renter or homeowner.

MY HOME	YES	NO
My home is in a location where I will not feel isolated in my later years and is close to services, friends, and family.		
I have thought about current and future costs of staying in my home (e.g., mortgage or rent, condo fees, taxes, repairs, maintenance) and whether I can afford to live there as I age.		
I can afford to pay for services (e.g., house cleaning, yard maintenance) to maintain my home, if needed.		
If I find myself living alone in the future, I could manage it on my own.		
I recognize safety risks in my home and have taken steps to fix them.		
I have spoken to my landlord or condo board to find out if changes can be made to my current home.		
The features in my home have been reviewed by a health professional to ensure they will adequately support my mobility and health needs over the next ten to fifteen years (e.g., entryways and doorways that can be accessed by a walker, bathroom walls that can support the installation handrails, etc.).		
In the future, I will make changes as needed to my home to help me to age in place (e.g., night lights in the stair areas, solid handrails on both sides of the staircase and a grab bar in the tub area).		
If my health changes and I need to use a wheelchair or another mobility device, I am prepared to modify my home to accommodate my needs (e.g., widen doorways, build a ramp, install a walk-in bathtub, employ assistive technologies).		
If I am no longer able to remain in my current home, I am aware of other available housing options in my community or other desirable communities, including applicable costs, funding, and waitlists.		
TOTAL of all YES and NO answers:		

MY TRANSPORTATION

Most older adults will live seven to ten years past their ability to drive safely.

Think about the type(s) of transportation you use now. Do you plan to continue traveling in the same way when you are older?

MY TRANSPORTATION	YES	NO
If I am able to continue driving, I plan to take a refresher course to maintain my skills and knowledge of the rules and regulations.		
I talk to my doctor or pharmacist about how my health conditions, and the medications used to manage them, can impact my ability to drive safely.		
I am aware of, and have access to, alternate means of transportation if needed (e.g., walking paths, bus routes, taxi, volunteer driving and carpool programs).		
I have thought about what it costs to run and maintain my own vehicle compared to the cost of other means of transportation.		
I plan to take up or increase walking or cycling as a healthy and active form of transportation.		
I am aware of delivery and online shopping services I can use if I am not able to travel.		
I have thought about my future transportation needs and would be willing to relocate so I can continue to have access to the services I need.		
TOTAL of all YES and NO answers:		

☀ MY FINANCES

Financial planning leads to greater well-being, regardless of household income.

Philosophia
—— WITHIN ——

Think about the state of your finances and your source(s) of income now. What will they be like when you are seventy to eighty years of age or older?

MY FINANCES	YES	NO
I am able to live comfortably within my current income.		
I have money set aside for unexpected expenses such as healthrelated supports and major home repairs.		
I have someone that I trust that I can consult for financial advice when needed. If not, I have a plan to interview at least three financial advisors.		
I have thought about my retirement, the kind of lifestyle I would like to have and I've calculated the total budget I need to afford that lifestyle.		
I have thought about the kinds of supports and services I may need to purchase as I age (e.g., cleaning, shopping, yard maintenance and personal care support).		
I am aware of all sources of income I will have or may become entitled to (e.g., employer pensions, investments, survivor or death benefits, old age security, government supplements or pensions, etc.).		
I plan to retire debt-free (e.g., pay off mortgage and credit cards).		
I know of ways I can transition to retirement that can maintain or increase my income (e.g., work part-time, become a consultant, retire early and try a new career, or start a business on the side and keep it going postretirement).		

MY FINANCES	YES	NO
I plan to have my retirement income based on more than one source (e.g., personal savings, Canada Pension Plan (CPP), Registered Retirement Savings Plan (RRSP/RRIF), Old Age Security (OAS), other pensions, investments or employment income).		
If my living arrangements changed, I could thrive, not simply survive, financially.		
I have a plan for who will be responsible for my financial affairs if I am not able to look after them myself (e.g., an enduring power of attorney) and have communicated my plan to those involved.		
I have a notarized will, and my loved ones know where all my important documents are (e.g., will, personal directive, power of attorney, insurance, etc.).		
I have an emergency savings fund of 3 to 6 months of my total income.		
I have considered and acquired all insurances to meet my needs. (e.g., critical Illness, life Insurance, medical Insurance, long-term care, etc.)		
TOTAL of all YES and NO answers:		

Check with your local government or speak to a lawyer to find out what laws are in place to allow someone else to have legal authority to manage your finances for you.

Needing help making legal and financial decisions can happen at any time and for a wide range of reasons. If you become ill, have an accident or are just away for a period of time, having someone you trust who is ready and able to help you can save time and trouble.

MY SOCIAL CONNECTIONS

The ability to draw on social networks of friends or family is known to make an important contribution to general well-being and quality of life. Volunteering helps to keep people connected with their community, is associated with longevity, and increases happiness and satisfaction in older age.

Think about your social life as it is now. What will it look like when you are older?

MY SOCIAL CONNECTIONS	YES	NO
I maintain good relationships with my family members.		
I have family/friends I can rely on for support if needed.		
I have someone I can talk to when I need to do so.		
I have friends I enjoy spending time with, and I nurture the friendships I have. If not, I have a plan to make new friends.		
I have friends who are of different ages, some of whom are younger than I am.		
I enjoy connecting with people through my work and plan to work full- or part-time for as long as I am able.		
I have built deeper relationships with some of my work colleagues whom I would like to stay connected with after I retire.		
I have developed social networks outside of my work.		
I have considered how I would like to stay connected with my community. (e.g., joining a club or community group)		
If my living arrangements changed, I could thrive, not just survive, socially.		
I may explore volunteering as a way to contribute to my community and provide social contact.		
I have explored different ways of connecting with friends and family, such as ZOOM, FaceTime, texting, social media, or other new assistive technologies. I am aware of agencies that can assist me with accessing and using technology if needed.		
TOTAL of all YES and NO answers:		

 ## MY SAFETY

Falls account for more than half of all injuries to Canadians sixty-five years of age and older. Approximately 20 to 30 percent of Canadian seniors experience one fall each year.

Think about some of the things you do now to protect yourself and reduce the potential for various types of injury, harm, or abuse. Might you have other safety concerns when you are older? What could you do to reduce the risk of these occurring?

MY SAFETY	YES	NO
I feel safe in my home and my neighbourhood.		
I know how to protect myself from abuse and neglect (including emotional, physical, and financial abuse or neglect).		
I know how to protect myself from frauds (door to door, online or over the phone) and what to do if I fall victim to one.		
I know falling is a risk, and I know what I can do to decrease this risk.		
I keep my home uncluttered by removing scatter rugs and other tripping hazards.		
I keep my walkway clear of snow and ice.		
I had a fall recently, but I took action to decrease my risk of having another.		
I have considered or am using a home monitoring system, personal emergency response system, or a fall detection system to help keep me safe at home. I know who to call in the event of an emergency.		
TOTAL of all YES and NO answers:		

MY SUPPORTS & SERVICES

SUPPORTS: You may already be caring for a parent, spouse, adult child, grandchild, or friend, or you may do so in the future. Think about how this role is affecting, or may effect, your life and what you might do that would help you in providing that care.

SERVICES: At some point in your life, you may need help with some activities or with some daily needs of living at home, such as housekeeping, yard work, or meal prep. Would you be able to manage if you could not do these activities for a short or long period of time?

MY SUPPORTS & SERVICES	YES	NO
I have thought about what services and supports I may need to remain in my home and thrive in the future.		
I know where to go to find information if I have questions about my care needs or community services.		
I have talked to family and friends about help I may need in the future, so they can prepare accordingly.		
I have thought of using devices such as a video monitoring system, medication reminders, and a personal response service to help me care for myself or a loved one at home.		
As a caregiver (or if I become a caregiver in the future), I know what resources and respite services are available to help me in this role.		
If I am a caregiver, I have a plan for self-care to help maintain my own health and well-being.		
TOTAL of all YES and NO answers:		

☀ MY COMMUNITY

In an age-friendly community, policies, services, and structures related to the physical and social environment are designed to support and enable older people to "age actively"—that is, to live in security, enjoy good health, and continue to participate fully in society.

Think about the community you live in now. How close are you to a grocery store, a pharmacy, a coffee shop, a library or a restaurant? How much farther do you travel to reach medical offices, a dentist or a hospital? How far do you travel to visit family and friends? What features are important to have in your community when you are older, and will your current community meet your future needs?

MY COMMUNITY	YES	NO
I am comfortable getting around in my community and will continue to be in the future.		
I feel safe in my community and know where to report concerns about how to make my community safer.		
I know what programs and services (e.g., shopping, personal services, health and support services, and recreation programs) are available in my community.		
There are activities in my community that interest me, and I know how to find out more about them.		
In the future, I may move to another community or to another area in my community that is better designed to help older adults to live safely, enjoy good health, and stay involved. This is called an "age-friendly" community.		
TOTAL of all YES and NO answers:		

MY PARTNER (& ME)

Your partner, if applicable, will play a critical role in your later years and will likely become a more central part of your life.

Think about your relationship with your partner as it is now. What changes might you anticipate as you age and your needs change?

MY PARTNER (& ME)	YES	NO
My partner and I have discussed our plans for retirement and our older years.		
MY PARTNER AND I HAVE SHARED OUR PLANS FOR:		
What we want to be able to do and how we want to live financially.		
When we will retire.		
What options we may explore to work part-time or in a new job.		
What we will do with our time. (e.g., volunteer, travel, meet friends).		
What activities we can do together and separately.		
How aging or changing needs could affect our relationship.		
Where we want to live that meets both our needs and preferences.		
How to nurture our relationship and work out any problems as our needs change.		
TOTAL of all YES and NO answers:		

LIVING & AGING WELL READINESS ASSESSMENT RESULTS

Transfer your total Yes/No responses from each section above to the checklist in this summary table.

Yes responses indicate those areas of your life where you are most prepared for the future. **No responses** indicate areas where you need more preparation to successfully age in place or to determine other suitable living options.

Review your No responses in each section. These are the areas you may wish to reflect upon and try to make changes. You can now proceed to the **Create Your Personal Action Plan** section to consider things you can do to be better prepared for a healthy future at home.

ASSESSMENT RESULTS	YES	NO
My Health (p.94-95)		
My Home (p.96)		
My Transportation (p.97)		
My Finances (p.98-99)		
My Social Connections (p.100)		
My Safety (p.101)		
My Supports & Services (p.102)		
My Community (p.103)		
My Partner (& Me) (p.104)		
TOTAL of all YES and NO answers:		

Let's Plan

Now that you have imagined your ideal future, learned about many options, and assessed your readiness to create it, let's get started planning. There is no time like the present to make your dreams and intentions come true.

"The best way to predict the future is to create it."
— **Peter Drucker**

Create Your Personal Action Plan

Use this section to develop your personal action plan with SMART goals—steps you can take now, and in the future, to better prepare for your later years. SMART stands for specific, measurable, achievable, relevant and time-bound.

Write down one goal from each life area that you can start working on now. You can refer back to it periodically to remind yourself about the steps you can take now to support your plans for aging in place in the future.

Here's an example of a **SMART goal**:

- **Goal:** I want to lower my blood pressure through regular physical activity so I can improve my heart health and reduce my risk of disease.
- **Specific:** I will walk for 30 minutes, five days a week, to help lower my blood pressure and strengthen my cardiovascular health.
- **Measurable:** I will track my walks with a fitness app and monitor my blood pressure weekly to see progress.
- **Achievable:** I can start with 15 minutes per walk and gradually build up to 30 minutes, fitting it into my lunch break or after dinner.
- **Relevant:** Improving my blood pressure is important for my long-term health and energy, and I'm ready to commit to this lifestyle change now.
- **Time-bound:** My goal is to consistently meet this walking routine for the next 12 weeks and lower my blood pressure by at least 5 points by the end of that period.

☀ PERSONAL ACTION PLAN

What Is a SMART Goal?
Specific — What do I want to accomplish and why?
Measurable — How will I know when I have accomplished it?
Achievable — How can I accomplish this goal?
Relevant — Is this the right time for me to be working toward this goal?
Time-bound — When do I want to accomplish this goal by?
Life Area: HEALTH
Specific —
Measurable —
Achievable —
Relevant —
Time-bound —
Life Area: HOME
Specific —
Measurable —
Achievable —
Relevant —
Time-bound —
Life Area: TRANSPORTATION
Specific —
Measurable —
Achievable —
Relevant —
Time-bound —

Philosophia
WITHIN

What Is a SMART Goal?
Specific — What do I want to accomplish and why?
Measurable — How will I know when I have accomplished it?
Achievable — How can I accomplish this goal?
Relevant — Is this the right time for me to be working toward this goal?
Time-bound — When do I want to accomplish this goal by?
Life Area: FINANCES
Specific —
Measurable —
Achievable —
Relevant —
Time-bound —
Life Area: SOCIAL CONNECTIONS
Specific —
Measurable —
Achievable —
Relevant —
Time-bound —
Life Area: SAFETY
Specific —
Measurable —
Achievable —
Relevant —
Time-bound —

What Is a SMART Goal?
Specific — What do I want to accomplish and why?
Measurable — How will I know when I have accomplished it?
Achievable — How can I accomplish this goal?
Relevant — Is this the right time for me to be working toward this goal?
Time-bound — When do I want to accomplish this goal by?
Life Area: SUPPORTS & SERVICES
Specific —
Measurable —
Achievable —
Relevant —
Time-bound —
Life Area: MY COMMUNITY
Specific —
Measurable —
Achievable —
Relevant —
Time-bound —
Life Area: MY PARTNER & ME
Specific —
Measurable —
Achievable —
Relevant —
Time-bound —

What Is a SMART Goal?
Specific — What do I want to accomplish and why?
Measurable — How will I know when I have accomplished it?
Achievable — How can I accomplish this goal?
Relevant — Is this the right time for me to be working toward this goal?
Time-bound — When do I want to accomplish this goal by?
Life Area:
Specific —
Measurable —
Achievable —
Relevant —
Time-bound —
Life Area:
Specific —
Measurable —
Achievable —
Relevant —
Time-bound —
Life Area:
Specific —
Measurable —
Achievable —
Relevant —
Time-bound —

Living Options Comparison Worksheet

Use this worksheet to compare different older adult living facilities during your tours. Make multiple copies. Fill in the blanks to help make an informed decision.

Facility Name	
Phone Number	
Location	
Website	
Waitlist Time	
Type of Facility (e.g., Independent Living, LTC)	
Contract Terms (Rental, Buy-In, etc.)	
Monthly Cost	
Service & Amenities Included	

Service & Amenities Extra $	
Pet Policy & Cost	
Vibe Rating (How did I feel here?) / 10 1=Uncomfortable 10=Feels like home	
Staff Friendliness & Helpfulness	
Resident Interactions & Atmosphere	
Cleanliness & Maintenance	
Food Quality (if Sampled)	
Meets My Current Needs / 10	
Can Adapt to My Future Needs /10	
Overall Thoughts & Final Rating / 10	
Additional Notes	
Next Steps	

Local Resources & Services

Collect local resources as referred to you by your health, social, or family & community support services providers and as you do your own research.

Service Provider	Type of Service	Contact/Details

Let's Be Proactive

Balance is the key—true wellness comes from balance across mind, body, soul, and spirit.

&

While life is unpredictable, being prepared is a gift of peace—to yourself, your loved ones, and those who may help you. Taking the time now to plan your estate and gather vital information empowers you to face the unexpected with control, confidence, and grace.

"Both faith and fear demand you to believe in something you cannot see and require energy. You choose."
— Kathleen Cesarin

A Balanced Path to Wholeness

To support you in beginning this journey, I've included a gentle introduction to practices that nourish the mind, body, soul, and spirit. This section offers introductory yet foundational wisdom to help you step into greater balance, awareness, and inner peace.

Together, let's journey toward health, authenticity and wholeness—keys to living and aging well.

☀ Mind Wellness

- **Stay curious and open-minded.** Keep learning, exploring, and questioning. Read widely, seek new experiences, and engage in meaningful conversations. A curious mind stays vibrant and resilient.

- **Challenge limiting beliefs.** Your thoughts shape your reality. What you believe becomes your truth and your reality, whether it's helpful to you or not. Recognize and release patterns of self-doubt and negative self-talk. Replace them with empowering affirmations that promote self-confidence and self-love.

- **Practice mindfulness and intentional stillness.** Meditate, breathe deeply, and embrace moments of quiet. This calms mental noise, bringing clarity and peace.

- **Discern truth wisely**. In a world filled with noise, disinformation, and division, be mindful of where you place your attention. Seek unbiased, reputable sources and stay open to diverse perspectives. Seek truth, not to be "right". Do not seek blind acceptance nor easy agreement.

- **Look upward and inward.** When confusion and chaos surround you, seek guidance from the Divine (Creator/God/Higher Power/Universe—by whatever name resonates with you) and trust your inner wisdom. It holds eternal truth and clarity. Practice stillness, prayer, and listening.

☀ Body Wellness

- **Keep moving.** Movement is life. Walk, stretch, dance, and stay as active as possible daily. Listen to your body—challenge it but don't ignore its need for rest or recovery.

- **Nourish with intention.** Choose whole, unmodified foods whenever possible. Grow your own or support local markets to access nutrient-dense, fresh produce. Eat mindfully and with gratitude.

- **Seek expert guidance.** Consult a naturopath or holistic practitioner for personalized wellness support, such as food sensitivity testing. Understanding how your body responds to specific foods can transform your health.

- **Connect with nature.** Go outside often—walk barefoot on the grass, breathe fresh air, and let the sun touch your skin. Nature is where it is often easiest to hear yourself and the Divine.

- **Limit harmful substances.** Reduce or eliminate alcohol, smoking, and all processed foods. Treat your body with reverence—it is your vessel for this life. Drink fresh water several times daily.

☀ Emotional Wellness

- **Feel to heal.** Allow yourself to feel deeply—joy, grief, anger, and love. Suppressed emotions stagnate or even poison the soul. Express them honestly and compassionately. Seek help if need.

- **Choose emotional balance.** Release grudges and practice forgiveness—not necessarily for others, but to be free. Letting go of emotional burdens creates space for peace, growth, and more love.

- **Surround yourself with uplifting energy.** Listen to mindful and uplifting music—it soothes emotions and shifts energy. Let songs of love, peace, and joy be your daily soundtrack.

- **Nurture meaningful connections.** Spend time with people who uplift you. Quality, authentic relationships enrich emotional health far more than surface-level interactions.

- **Be kind to yourself.** Treat yourself with patience and compassion. Embrace self-love as a daily practice, not as a reward for perfection. Self-love is not being selfish, it's simply honoring you.

☀ Soul Wellness

- **Live with intention and reciprocity.** Your life is a sacred gift. Honor it by living with purpose, kindness, and gratitude. Give generously and receive humbly.

- **Trust your inner compass.** Your soul carries infinite wisdom. Trust its quiet whispers, even when the world is loud. Ask for wisdom from your Higher Power. Seek truth, not ego or acceptance.

- **Seek the sacred in the ordinary.** Find holiness and beauty in small moments—in shared laughter, a sunrise, or a stranger's smile. The Divine reveals itself in simplicity.

- **Practice surrender.** Let go of what you cannot control—people's opinions, politics, or global chaos. Focus on what you can influence: your thoughts, actions, and reactions.
- **Radiate peace and unity.** When uncertainty and fear dominate the world, choose calm. Act with wisdom, kindness, and peace. Seek unity over division—it is the path to wholeness.

☀ Balance Is the Key

- **True wellness comes from balance across mind, body, soul, and spirit.** When one is neglected, the whole being suffers. Find balance while being true to your authentic self.
- **Advocate for yourself.** In your healthcare journey, don't hesitate to seek second or third opinions. Trust your instincts and consider blending traditional medicine with alternative therapies.
- **Honor your wholeness.** You are not just a body, nor just a mind—you are a radiant being with a soul. Caring for yourself in all aspects is the ultimate act of self-love.

☀ A Gentle Reminder

You were created whole and beautiful—a being of light, wisdom, and love. Care for yourself with reverence. When you nourish your mind, body, emotions, and soul in harmony, you honor the gift of life and become a beacon of healing and hope for those around you. **You. Are. Loved.** 🌿❤️🌺

The Power of Good Sleep Hygiene

☀ Rest Well. Live Well. Heal Deeply.

Getting six to eight hours of restful sleep nightly is essential to physical health, emotional well-being, mental clarity, and spiritual renewal. Good sleep hygiene—daily habits and choices that support restful sleep—can prevent chronic illness, reduce stress, and enhance longevity.

☀ Why Sleep Matters

- **Memory & Brain Health:** Sleep consolidates memories and flushes toxins from the brain.
- **Immune Function:** Quality sleep strengthens immune response.
- **Emotional Regulation:** Sleep supports mood and resilience.
- **Cellular Repair**: Deep sleep allows the body to repair muscles and tissues.

☀ Key Sleep Hygiene Tips

Stick to a Consistent Sleep Schedule

Wake up at the same time daily—even on weekends. This resets your circadian rhythm, teaching your body when to wind down and when to wake up.

Avoid These Six to Eight Hours Before Bed:

- **Caffeine** – Blocks sleep-inducing adenosine.
- **Nicotine** – A stimulant that disrupts REM sleep.
- **Alcohol** – May make you drowsy, but fragments sleep cycles.

Wind Down Before Bed:

- Turn off screens at least one hour before bed.
- Avoid stimulating conversations or tasks.
- Try meditation, deep breathing exercises, gentle stretching, reading, or journaling.

Tip: "Dump" your thoughts onto paper. Release racing worries, to-do lists, and emotional tensions.

Try Soothing Rituals:

- A warm bath or shower helps lower your core body temperature and signals the brain it's time to sleep.

Create a Sleep-Friendly Bedroom:

- Cool, dark, and quiet (ideal temp: 16–19°C / 60–67°F).
- Use supportive pillows and comfortable bedding.

- Remove light and noise, or use a white noise machine if needed.

Mind Your Meals:

- Eat a light snack if hungry, but avoid: chocolate, peanuts, beans, raw veggies, spicy or fatty foods (gas or indigestion).

- Avoid heavy meals or middle-of-the-night snacking.

- Don't go to bed too hungry or overly full.

Sleep Tips That Work

- Exercise regularly—preferably early in the day.

- Avoid naps after 3:00 p.m.

- Limit time in bed—if not asleep in fifteen to twenty minutes, get up and do something relaxing.

- Learn to distinguish tiredness (low energy) from sleepiness (yawning, eye-drooping)—only the latter leads to sleep.

Holistic Approaches for the "Night Season"

Think of bedtime as the beginning of your day, not the end.

- Set a positive intention for tomorrow as you drift off.

- Actively surrender fears, anxieties, and control.

- Speak kindly to yourself: "I am safe. I am loved. I am held. Tomorrow will unfold for my highest good."

- Ask your inner wisdom or higher power to restore, guide, and renew you through sleep and intentional dreaming.

☀ Sleep Is Not Just Rest—It's Recovery

Your mind, body, and spirit process, restore, and realign while you sleep. Prioritize it like you would any other form of healing.

Unlocking Your Inner Potential: An Introduction to Meditation and Breathwork

You have within you the power to transform your mind, body, and life. The key lies in aligning your inner world— your thoughts, emotions, and energy—with the potential of who you want to become. Meditation and breathwork are powerful tools to help you shift from survival to creation, from the known past into the unknown possibilities of your future self. When we meditate, we step beyond the noise of our daily routines and conditioned patterns. We enter the present moment—a timeless space where transformation begins.

Breathwork enhances this process by regulating the nervous system, calming the mind, and drawing energy up the spine, helping awaken dormant potential and elevate consciousness.

Getting Started: A Simple Daily Practice

1. Create Your Space

Find a quiet, comfortable space where you won't be disturbed. Sit upright or lie down, spine straight, hands resting gently.

2. Set an Intention

Before you begin, ask yourself: Who do I want to be today? Set a clear intention or elevated emotion— such as gratitude, joy, or love—to focus on during your meditation.

3. Begin with Breathwork (Three to Five minutes)

- Inhale slowly through your nose, filling your lungs fully.
- At the top of the breath, gently contract your lower abdomen, pulling energy up from your base.

- Imagine this breath and energy rising up your spine to the top of your head.
- Exhale slowly through your mouth, relaxing your body.
- Repeat, focusing your awareness inward.

4. Meditate (Ten to twenty minutes)

- Shift your attention away from your external world—your body, time, and environment.
- Focus on the space behind your eyes or in your heart's center.
- Stay open and present. If thoughts arise, gently return your focus to your breath or intention.
- Allow yourself to feel the elevated emotion you set earlier. Let it expand.

5. Close with Gratitude

Before opening your eyes, thank yourself for showing up. Let gratitude seal the practice.

With regular practice, you can begin to rewire your brain, regulate your emotions, and tap into new levels of awareness. You are not defined by your past. You are empowered to create a new future—starting now, from within.

Dreaming the Way Through Aging

"Dreams come to unhinge our fixed positions."
– Pearl Gregor, PhD

Dr. Pearl Gregor describes herself as a dream coach, writer, and Crone of wisdom—a woman who has walked through the darkness of depression and emerged with insights that resonate deeply with those navigating aging, loss, and personal reinvention. Now in her eighties, Pearl continues to guide others in exploring the landscape of their inner lives, championing the transformative power of dreams, storytelling, and reflection.

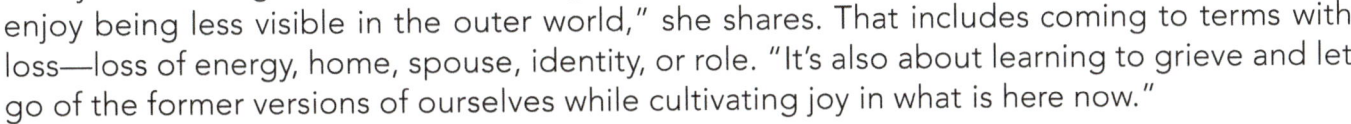

For Pearl, aging well means embracing change with curiosity and courage. "It means learning to live with and enjoy being less visible in the outer world," she shares. That includes coming to terms with loss—loss of energy, home, spouse, identity, or role. "It's also about learning to grieve and let go of the former versions of ourselves while cultivating joy in what is here now."

Pearl encourages creating a "Conscious Dying Plan" by making use of the information, tools and worksheets in this *Living and Aging Well* book and sharing it with close family and friends. "Taking ownership of our final chapter is not morbid," she insists. "It's empowering." She also recommends writing and sharing one's life story. "Your Memoir Album or Life Story is a gift to your loved ones—a legacy of wisdom."

Dreams: A Lifeline Out of Depression

Pearl's journey into dreamwork began in 1988 at age forty-two, as a last-ditch effort to heal from decades of depression that began when she was just nine. A meditation group opened the door, and then, serendipitously, a box of books from her concerned brother's wife arrived. One of them, *A Christian Approach to Dreamwork*, lit a spark.

"I read it that same night," she recalls. "It said I could ask for a dream. So, I did." On December 11, 1988, she received a dream she later titled "The Descent to Inanna". That single dream marked the beginning of her healing and an entirely new chapter in life. "It was like the Creator reached into my soul and handed me a map," Pearl says. "That dream has propelled me for thirty-seven years."

☀ How to Begin Dreamwork

Pearl insists anyone can begin working with their dreams. Here's how:

1. Create a sacred space: Keep a notebook or special dream journal beside your bed, along with a pen.

2. Ask for a dream: As you drift off, repeat, "I will remember a dream tonight."

3. Write immediately: Upon waking, stay in bed and mentally replay your dream. Then write it down quickly and without censorship.

4. Use your own symbolism: "Do *not* use a dream dictionary," Pearl warns. "You know the meaning of your dream symbols. Begin by exploring the nouns and asking what they mean to you."

5. Share cautiously: Share your dream only with one trusted confidant who respects the sacredness of the process.

Pearl has also created tools to support others on this journey, including her Dream Manual and Dream Journal, both available on Amazon. Her website, **www.dreamsalongtheway.com**, offers articles, mythic references, and dream interpretation guidance.

☀ Myth and Archetype: The Inanna Story

Pearl's dreamwork is deeply influenced by mythology, particularly the ancient Sumerian myth of Inanna, a goddess who descends into the underworld, faces death, and returns renewed. Inanna passes through seven gates, each requiring her to shed a piece of her identity, until she is stripped bare and left hanging for three days. Empathy arrives in the form of tiny flies, and Inanna is eventually reborn.

"This myth became a mirror of my own descent," Pearl explains. "My dream began with me landing in lamb's wool or chicken feathers—earth symbols that told me I was safe, loved, and ready for deep inner work." These mythic patterns offer comfort and guidance during transitions, especially for older adults navigating grief, loss, and the shedding of former identities. "We must go inward, meet the Shadow, and come out the other side," she says.

☀ Writing, Journaling, and Generative Reflection

Pearl is a prolific journaler. Her practice involves more than just recording dreams; it includes:

- Daily generative writing (new ideas, questions, observations)
- Recording snippets of conversations
- Reading, questioning, and integrating wisdom from books
- Creating monthly collages from dream imagery

"Your journal becomes part of who you are," she says. "Bring it everywhere. Use it to notice repeating symbols or patterns. These are the breadcrumbs to your transformation." She also encourages sharing stories aloud in a community. Her Dream Readers' Myth Circle is one such space, where dreamers reflect, learn, and hold space for each other. "These groups create a soul connection," she explains. "They keep you accountable to your inner work."

For the Skeptical and the Curious

To those who are skeptical but curious, Pearl gently offers, "Begin now. Buy a journal. Say, 'I will remember a dream tonight.' Write it down. That's all. Let the process unfold." She adds, "Dreams of death are not prophetic. They tell us that a part of us is changing, not ending. Loved ones may come in dreams to remind us of love. Pay attention."

Never Too Late to Begin

Pearl is emphatic: "It is never, ever too late. Aging doesn't mean your spiritual work is done. Quite the opposite. This is the time to go inward, find meaning, and reclaim your soul." Now facing mobility limitations herself, Pearl acknowledges the difficulty of change. "My identity was tied up in being active," she reflects. "I had to grieve that loss, then choose to stand upright, face the storm, and embrace what I have learned. The past cannot be undone. The future is here to be lived. Change is inevitable. Live the change."

An Invitation to Inner Wisdom

For those caring for others—or caring for themselves—Pearl's message is clear: Your soul is still speaking, and dreams are one of its languages. In every stage of life, we are invited to listen more deeply, grieve more fully, and grow more courageously. "Dreams are the soul's language," Pearl says. "And the Crone's journey is not an ending—it's a beginning."

To learn more about Pearl Gregor's work, visit **www.dreamsalongtheway.com**.

Creating a Financially Secure Future: Intentional Steps to Age Well

Aging is a gift, but for many, the thought of financial preparedness for retirement can feel overwhelming. If you're in your forties, fifties, or even early sixties and find yourself anxious about the road ahead, know this: You are not alone, and it is never too late to take control of your financial future. By becoming intentional and mindful about financial planning today, you can create a future that supports not only your needs but also the life you truly desire.

The Urgency of Financial Preparedness

Many older adults worry about outliving their savings, rising healthcare costs, and maintaining their quality of life. Without a plan, these concerns can become real obstacles. However, with **awareness, action, and small, consistent steps, financial security can be within reach**—regardless of your current financial standing.

Key Steps to Take Control of Your Financial Future

1. Assess Where You Are Now

Start by getting an honest snapshot of your financial situation. Review your savings, income sources, investments, and debts. Many people avoid this step due to fear, but knowledge is power. Clarity will help you make informed decisions.

2. Reduce Debt & Live Within Your Means

High-interest debt, such as credit cards, can erode your financial future. Develop a plan to eliminate or reduce debt while making mindful spending choices. Downsizing your home, cutting unnecessary subscriptions, or reevaluating expenses can free up cash for savings.

3. Maximize Savings & Retirement Contributions

Even if you started late, contributing consistently to retirement accounts like RRSPs, TFSAs, 401(k)s, or IRAs can make a significant difference. If your employer offers matching contributions, take full advantage of them. Every dollar saved now compounds over time.

4. Create Additional Income Streams

Explore ways to supplement your income, whether through part-time work, consulting, renting out a portion of your home, or turning a hobby into a small business. Passive income from investments or rental properties can also be a long-term strategy.

5. Plan for Healthcare & Long-Term Care

Unexpected health expenses can be financially devastating. Look into insurance options, government benefits, and savings strategies that can help cover medical needs as you age. Prioritizing health through preventive care can also reduce costs in the long run.

6. Reimagine Your Retirement Lifestyle

Many envision retirement as an expensive endeavor, but with creativity, it doesn't have to be. Consider cost-effective living arrangements such as cohousing, relocating to an area with a lower cost of living, or engaging in community-based programs that offer affordable resources.

7. Seek Professional Guidance

A financial planner, lawyer, and accountant can help you navigate complex financial decisions, ensuring your plan aligns with your goals.

8. Inventory Your Assets & Update Essential Documents

Ask your advisors if there are tax advantages to retitling your assets and reorganizing your finances in a different way as you age and plan your estate.

A Call to Action: Start Today

Financial security doesn't happen overnight, but small, intentional actions today can lead to a secure and fulfilling future. Whether you begin by reducing a single expense, increasing your savings by a few dollars, or reaching out for professional advice, every step counts. Your later years should be a time of peace, joy, and purpose. By taking control of your finances now, you can design the life you desire and embrace the years ahead with confidence. The power to create your financial future is in your hands—start today!

 ## Melissa's Journey: From Fear to Financial Freedom

Melissa, fifty-two, had spent the last decade rebuilding her life after a difficult divorce. With no significant savings and a home to maintain, she often lay awake at night worrying about her future. The thought of financially burdening her children terrified her. She longed for a secure retirement and even dreamed of traveling, but without a plan, those dreams seemed distant. Anxiety, fear, and self-doubt consumed her, making it difficult to take action.

One day, after yet another sleepless night, Melissa decided enough was enough. Her friend recommended she reach out to a reputable, experienced financial advisor for a customized evaluation of her situation.

During her first meeting, she felt vulnerable but hopeful. The financial planner helped her assess her income, debt, and future needs. Together, they created a step-by-step plan tailored to her goals.

She started by setting up a budget that prioritized savings and cut unnecessary expenses. She refinanced her mortgage to lower her monthly payments, allowing her to contribute more to her retirement fund. She also explored part-time work opportunities that fit her lifestyle, providing her with extra income without sacrificing her health. Most importantly, she learned how to make her money work for her by investing wisely and preparing for future healthcare costs.

As the months passed, Melissa's anxiety transformed into confidence. Seeing her savings grow and her plan unfold gave her a renewed sense of purpose. She no longer felt paralyzed by fear; instead, she felt empowered by the steps she was taking.

Now, Melissa looks forward to her retirement years with excitement. She no longer sees the future as uncertain and frightening but as a chapter she is actively creating. With each intentional step, she moves closer to financial security and the fulfilling, worry-free life she deserves.

Estate Planning: Why It Matters and How to Get Started

Estate planning ensures your wishes are respected regarding your finances, healthcare, and personal affairs in case of illness, incapacity, or death. A complete estate plan includes a will, power of attorney, personal directive, and an end-of-life plan. These documents provide clarity and peace of mind for both you and your loved ones.

☀ Key Components of an Estate Plan

Will: Specifies how your assets will be distributed upon your passing and appoints an executor to manage your estate.

Power of Attorney: Grants someone authority to handle your financial affairs if you are unable to do so.

Personal Directive (Living Will): Outlines your medical and personal care preferences if you become incapacitated.

End-of-Life Plan: Details your wishes regarding funeral arrangements, organ donation, and other final decisions.

☀ How to Create These Documents for Free or at a Low Cost

Government Resources: Many jurisdictions provide free or low-cost templates for wills, powers of attorney, and personal directives.

Legal Aid Services: Some nonprofit organizations offer estate planning assistance to low-income individuals.

Online Templates: Legal Aid, Law Depot, provincial/state legal websites, and some financial institutions offer free or low-cost legal forms.

Community Workshops: Local senior centers, libraries, and community organizations often hold free estate planning workshops.

Check Local Laws: Estate planning laws vary by province, state, territory and country. Ensure your documents comply with your local regulations to be legally valid.

☀ Benefits of Estate Planning

Control Over Asset Distribution: Ensures your assets are distributed according to your wishes, preventing unintended beneficiaries from inheriting your estate.

Family Harmony: Reduces family disputes and legal complications by providing clear instructions on asset distribution and personal care decisions.

Protection in Incapacity: Appoints a trusted person to handle your affairs if you become incapacitated, ensuring that your financial and healthcare decisions align with your wishes.

Medical Decision Clarity: Provides clear instructions for medical decisions, including end-of-life care, reducing stress and uncertainty for loved ones.

Cost and Time Savings: Saves time and money by avoiding costly probate and legal fees, ensuring a smooth transition for your beneficiaries.

Peace of Mind: Allows you to make informed decisions in advance, relieving your family from the burden of making difficult choices during emotionally challenging times.

☀ Risks of Not Having an Estate Plan

State/Province-Controlled Distribution: Your assets may be distributed based on provincial/state intestacy laws, which may not align with your wishes and could exclude important individuals from inheriting.

Family Conflict and Legal Battles: Without a will, disputes among family members may arise, leading to lengthy and costly legal proceedings that can strain relationships.

Loss of Control Over Healthcare Decisions: If incapacitated, decisions about your finances and healthcare may be left to court-appointed individuals rather than someone you trust, potentially resulting in unwanted medical treatments or financial mismanagement.

Higher Legal Costs and Delays: The probate process can become more expensive and time- consuming without a clear estate plan, depleting assets that would otherwise go to beneficiaries.

Financial Burden on Loved Ones: Without clear instructions on funeral expenses and estate administration, loved ones may struggle to cover costs and manage your affairs.

Risk of Fraud or Mismanagement: Without legal safeguards, unscrupulous individuals may take advantage of your estate, leading to potential financial loss for your heirs.

Will Planning Questions

Preparing a will can be a complex but is an essential task. Here are fifteen key questions to ask yourself to facilitate the process:

1. **Who will be my executor?** Choose someone trustworthy to manage and distribute your estate according to your wishes.

2. **Who are my beneficiaries?** List the people or organizations (e.g., charities) that will inherit your assets.

3. **What assets do I own?** Consider real estate, bank accounts, investments, personal belongings, and digital assets.

4. **Do I have any debts or liabilities?** Determine how outstanding debts, loans, or taxes will be handled.

5. **Who will be the guardian for my minor children?** If you have children under eighteen, decide who will care for them.

6. **Do I want to leave specific gifts or personal belongings to certain people?** Outline any sentimental or valuable items you want to pass on.

7. **How do I want my final arrangements to be handled?** Specify burial, cremation, or other funeral preferences.

8. **What happens if a beneficiary or executor predeceases me?** Consider alternative beneficiaries and backup executors.

9. **Do I need to set up a trust?** If you have dependents with special needs or young beneficiaries, a trust might be useful.

10. **Have I reviewed and updated beneficiary designations on accounts?** Ensure life insurance, pensions, and other accounts align with your will.

11. **Do I have business interests that need to be addressed?** If you own a business, decide how it will be managed, transferred, or dissolved.

12. **Have I considered tax implications for my estate and beneficiaries?** Understand potential estate taxes and ways to minimize their impact.

13. **Do I need to include provisions for pets?** If you have pets, consider who will care for them and if funds should be set aside.

14. **Who will have access to my digital assets and online accounts?** Decide how you want email, social media, and financial accounts to be handled.

15. **Have I communicated my wishes to my loved ones?** While not legally necessary, discussing your will with key people can prevent confusion or disputes.

Power of Attorney Questions

Choosing a power of attorney (POA) is a significant decision. Here are fifteen important questions to ask yourself when selecting a POA and defining their responsibilities:

☀ Choosing the Right Power of Attorney

1. **Who do I trust to make important decisions on my behalf?** This person should be reliable and responsible and have your best interests at heart.

2. **Should I choose one person or multiple people?** Consider if one POA is sufficient or if you need coagents to share responsibilities.

3. **Do I want my POA to be a family member, friend, or a professional (e.g., lawyer, accountant)?** Each option has pros and cons based on relationships and expertise.

4. **Does my chosen POA have the time and willingness to take on this role?** Managing your affairs can be time-consuming, so ensure they are available and capable.

5. **Does my POA understand my values, priorities, and preferences?** They should be able to make decisions that align with your wishes.

6. **Should I appoint a backup (alternate) POA?** In case your first choice is unable or unwilling to serve, having a backup is a good idea.

7. **Is my POA comfortable handling legal and financial matters?** They should be confident in managing money, paying bills, and making legal decisions.

8. **Do I need a general, limited, or enduring power of attorney?** A general POA covers all affairs, a limited POA is for specific tasks, and an enduring POA remains in effect if you become incapacitated.

9. **Do I want my POA to take effect immediately or only if I become incapacitated?** A "springing" POA activates only under certain conditions, while an immediate POA takes effect upon signing.

10. **How can I ensure my POA follows my instructions and does not misuse their power?** Consider adding oversight measures, requiring reports, or appointing a coagent.

☀ Defining Their Tasks and Responsibilities

1. **What financial decisions will my POA be responsible for?** Examples include paying bills, managing investments, filing taxes, and handling real estate.

2. **Should my POA have authority over my healthcare decisions?** A separate healthcare POA or advance directive may be needed for medical choices.

3. **Will my POA handle business affairs, if applicable?** If you own a business, specify whether they can manage operations or make financial decisions for it.

4. **Do I want my POA to make gifts or donations on my behalf?** Some people allow their POA to give charitable donations or financial gifts to family members.

5. **How will I update or revoke my POA if my circumstances change?** Ensure you know the legal process to modify or cancel your POA if needed.

Personal Directive Questions

A personal directive (also known as a living will or advance directive) outlines your healthcare and personal care wishes if you become unable to make decisions. Here are fifteen key questions to consider when preparing one:

☀ Choosing a Decision-Maker (Agent or Proxy)

1. **Who do I trust to make healthcare and personal care decisions on my behalf?** This should be someone who understands and respects your values.

2. **Should I appoint a backup decision-maker?** If your primary agent is unavailable, a backup ensures your wishes are still followed.

3. **Does my chosen agent understand my medical and personal care preferences?** They should be familiar with your beliefs and what matters most to you.

4. **Is my agent comfortable making difficult decisions under pressure?** They may need to make life- altering choices on your behalf.

5. **Should my agent have full decision-making authority or be limited to specific areas?** You can allow broad powers or specify certain treatments they can/cannot approve.

☀ Medical Treatment and Care Preferences

1. **What life-sustaining treatments do I want or not want?** Consider resuscitation (CPR), ventilators, dialysis, and artificial nutrition/hydration.

2. **Under what conditions would I want life support to continue or be withdrawn?** For example, irreversible coma, terminal illness, or severe brain injury.

3. **Do I want pain management and palliative care, even if it may shorten my life?** Some people prioritize comfort over life extension.

4. **Do I want to donate my organs or tissues?** Specify if you wish to be an organ donor and for which purposes (transplant, research, etc.).

5. **What are my preferences for mental healthcare if I become incapacitated?** Consider psychiatric treatment, therapy, or medications.

☀ Personal and End-of-Life Preferences

1. **Where do I want to receive care if I become seriously ill?** At home, in a hospital, hospice, or long-term care facility?

2. **Who should be informed and involved in my care decisions?** Decide if family, friends, or spiritual advisors should be consulted.

3. **Are there religious, cultural, or personal beliefs that should guide my care?** Certain faiths or traditions may influence medical treatments and end-of-life choices.

4. **What kind of funeral or memorial arrangements do I want?** Consider burial, cremation, specific religious services, or other instructions.

5. **How often should I review and update my directive?** Your wishes may change over time, so regular updates ensure accuracy.

End-of-Life Final Arrangements

Philosophia
— WITHIN —

Full Name:	
Date of Birth:	
Address:	
Funeral or Memorial Service Preferences:	
Funeral Home of Choice:	
Preferred Officiant (e.g., clergy, family member, friend):	
Burial or Cremation:	
Open or Closed Casket:	
Music Selections:	
Readings, Poems, or Eulogies:	

Reception or Gathering After the Service:	
Budget and Source of Funding for Arrangements:	
Private or Public Services (pre- or post-funeral):	
Prepaid Funeral Plan Details (if applicable):	
Invitees (Who do you want or not want to attend):	
Preferred Attire for Service (formal, casual, specific outfit):	
Flowers and Décor Preferences:	
Organ Donation:	

Grab and Go Vital Records Organizer

Philosophia
— WITHIN —

Take the time to complete the worksheets on pages 139–156. Doing this now will reduce stress in a crisis, give you peace of mind, and make it easier for helping professionals to support you.

Steps:

1. **Complete the worksheets** with your vital health, safety, and personal information. Make extra copies as needed.
2. **Store them in a safe, easily accessible location** (such as a folder, binder, a safe or emergency kit).
3. **Inform a trusted loved one** where these documents are kept, or give them a copy.
4. **Review and update the information regularly** to keep it accurate.

Why this matters:

By preparing in advance, you spare yourself and your loved ones unnecessary stress during an emergency and ensure first responders and professionals can assist you more effectively. You will thank yourself later for taking the time.

Emergency Contacts

Philosophia
— WITHIN —

EMERGENCY HOTLINE		FIRE DEPARTMENT	
Mobile:		Mobile:	
Telephone:		Telephone:	
Email:		Email:	
POISON CONTROL CENTER		POLICE DEPARTMENT	
Mobile:		Mobile:	
Telephone:		Telephone:	
Email:		Email:	
HOSPITAL EMERGENCY		PHARMACY	
Mobile:		Mobile:	
Telephone:		Telephone:	
Email:		Email:	
FAMILY DOCTOR		VETERINARIAN	
Mobile:		Mobile:	
Telephone:		Telephone:	
Email:		Email:	
ANIMAL CONTROL		INSURANCE	
Mobile:		Mobile:	
Telephone:		Telephone:	
Email:		Email:	

Personal Information

Philosophia
WITHIN

KEEP THIS INFORMATION CONFIDENTIAL, PRIVATE, AND SECURED AT ALL TIMES

FAMILY MEMBER			
DATE OF BIRTH			
PLACE OF BIRTH			
SIN / SSN			
PROV / STATE HEALTHCARE #			
PASSPORT NUMBER			
DRIVERS LICENSE NUMBER			
PHONE PIN / PASSWORD			

Medical Information

Philosophia
— WITHIN —

PERSONAL INFORMATION		
DATE OF BIRTH:	BIRTHPLACE:	BIRTHMARKS / SCARS:
WEIGHT:	EYE COLOR:	
HEIGHT:	CONTACTS:	HEALTH BENEFIT POLICY:
BLOOD TYPE:	EYEGLASSES:	

MY MEDICATIONS AND SUPPLEMENTS		
MEDICATION / SUPPLEMENT	TAKEN FOR	DOSAGE

FOOD, DRUG AND OTHER ALLERGIES		
ALLERGIES	TREATMENTS	NOTES

Doctor Visits

Philosophia
— WITHIN —

DATE	TIME
Doctor:	
Reason for visit:	
Question(s) to ask:	
Preparation(s):	
Next appointment:	

DATE	TIME
Doctor:	
Reason for visit:	
Question(s) to ask:	
Preparation(s):	
Next appointment:	

Online Accounts Tracker

Philosophia
WITHIN

WEBSITE / ACCOUNT:
EMAIL:
USERNAME:
PASSWORD:
NOTES:

WEBSITE / ACCOUNT:
EMAIL:
USERNAME:
PASSWORD:
NOTES:

WEBSITE / ACCOUNT:
EMAIL:
USERNAME:
PASSWORD:
NOTES:

WEBSITE / ACCOUNT:
EMAIL:
USERNAME:
PASSWORD:
NOTES:

WEBSITE / ACCOUNT:
EMAIL:
USERNAME:
PASSWORD:
NOTES:

WEBSITE / ACCOUNT:
EMAIL:
USERNAME:
PASSWORD:
NOTES:

WEBSITE / ACCOUNT:
EMAIL:
USERNAME:
PASSWORD:
NOTES:

WEBSITE / ACCOUNT:
EMAIL:
USERNAME:
PASSWORD:
NOTES:

Important Contacts: Family and Friends

Philosophia
— WITHIN —

CONTACT 1

NAME:

PHONE:

EMAIL:

ADDRESS:

CONTACT 2

NAME:

PHONE:

EMAIL:

ADDRESS:

CONTACT 3

NAME:

PHONE:

EMAIL:

ADDRESS:

CONTACT 4

NAME:

PHONE:

EMAIL:

ADDRESS:

CONTACT 5

NAME:

PHONE:

EMAIL:

ADDRESS:

CONTACT 6

NAME:

PHONE:

EMAIL:

ADDRESS:

CONTACT 7

NAME:

PHONE:

EMAIL:

ADDRESS:

CONTACT 8

NAME:

PHONE:

EMAIL:

ADDRESS:

Important Contacts: Personal Advisors

Philosophia
WITHIN

EXECUTOR
NAME:
PHONE:
EMAIL:
ADDRESS:

POWER OF ATTORNEY
NAME:
PHONE:
EMAIL:
ADDRESS:

PERSONAL DIRECTIVE
NAME:
PHONE:
EMAIL:
ADDRESS:

FINANCIAL
NAME:
PHONE:
EMAIL:
ADDRESS:

LAWYER
NAME:
PHONE:
EMAIL:
ADDRESS:

ACCOUNTANT
NAME:
PHONE:
EMAIL:
ADDRESS:

SPIRITUAL
NAME:
PHONE:
EMAIL:
ADDRESS:

OTHER
NAME:
PHONE:
EMAIL:
ADDRESS:

Important Contacts: Health Providers

Philosophia
— WITHIN —

FAMILY DOCTOR
NAME:

PHONE:

EMAIL:

ADDRESS:

DENTIST
NAME:

PHONE:

EMAIL:

ADDRESS:

SPECIALIST
NAME:

PHONE:

EMAIL:

ADDRESS:

SPECIALIST
NAME:

PHONE:

EMAIL:

ADDRESS:

SPECIALIST
NAME:

PHONE:

EMAIL:

ADDRESS:

THERAPIST
NAME:

PHONE:

EMAIL:

ADDRESS:

OPTOMETRIST
NAME:

PHONE:

EMAIL:

ADDRESS:

OTHER
NAME:

PHONE:

EMAIL:

ADDRESS:

Important Documents Tracker

Philosophia
WITHIN

	DOCUMENT	LOCATION	COPY LOCATION
1	WILLS		
2	PERSONAL DIRECTIVE		
3	POWER OF ATTORNEY		
4	BIRTH CERTIFICATES		
5	CITIZENSHIP / IMMIGRATION		
6	SOCIAL INSURANCE / SECURITY		
7	DRIVERS LICENCE / PHOTO ID		
8	MARRIAGE CERTIFICATE		
9	PASSPORTS		
10	INCOME TAX RETURNS		
11	VETERINARY RECORDS		
12	GRAB & GO VITAL RECORDS ORGANIZER		
13			
14			
15			
16			
17			
18			
19			
20			

Subscriptions Tracker

Philosophia
WITHIN

	SUBSCRIPTION / MEMBERSHIP (E.G., AMA, COSTCO, MAGAZINES, ETC.)	RENEWAL FREQUENCY	PAID BY
1			
2			
3			
4			
5			
6			
7			
8			
9			
10			
11			
12			
13			
14			
15			
16			
17			
18			
19			
20			

Financial Accounts Tracker

Philosophia
WITHIN

	TYPE: LOANS / PENSIONS / BANK ACCOUNTS / CREDIT CARDS / INVESTMENTS	PROVIDER / BANK	DETAILS	PAYMENT INFO
1				
2				
3				
4				
5				
6				
7				
8				
9				
10				
11				
12				
13				
14				
15				
16				
17				
18				
19				
20				

Insurances Tracker

Philosophia
— WITHIN —

	TYPE	PROVIDER	DETAILS	PAYMENT INFO
1	HOUSE / PROPERTY			
2	VEHICLE 1:			
3	VEHICLE 2:			
4	VEHICLE 3:			
5	VEHICLE 4:			
6	MORTGAGE			
7	CREDIT CARD / FRAUD			
8	LIFE INSURANCE			
9	RETIREE GROUP			
10	HEALTH / DENTAL			
11	CRITICAL ILLNESS			
12	ACCIDENTAL DEATH			
13				
14				
15				
16				
17				
18				
19				
20				

Other Household Trackers

Philosophia
— WITHIN —

UTILITIES	PAPER/EMAILED / AUTO PAYMENT	DETAILS	PAYMENT INFO
ELECTRICITY			
WATER / SEWER			
HEAT			

INCOME TAX RETURNS	PREPARED BY	DOCUMENTS LOCATION	YEARS

SAFETY DEPOSIT BOX	LOCATION	CONTENTS	

Medication and Health History

Philosophia
WITHIN

VET DETAILS	
VET NAME	
ADDRESS	
PHONE NUMBER	
EMAIL	
WEBSITE	

VACCINATION LOG		
VACCINATION	LOCATION	DATE

MEDICATION HISTORY		
MEDICATION	REASON	TIME & DOSAGE

My Pet Journal

Philosophia
WITHIN

OWNER:	
BASIC INFORMATION	
NAME	
DOB	
AGE	
GENDER	
BREED	
WEIGHT	
LENGTH	
NOTES	

DAILY ROUTINE			
BRAND OF FOOD		MEDICINES	
EAT TIME			
SLEEP TIME		ALLERGIES	
PLAY TIME			
WALK TIME			

OBSERVATIONS		
APPROVES	DISAPPROVES	CALMS

Don't Forget:
Stuff For Carry-On Bag

Philosophia
— WITHIN —

O **Travel Documents**	O **Clothes**
O **Prescription Medications**	O **Personal Toiletries**
O **Sleeping Aids**	O **Electronics**
O **Entertainment**	O **Valuables**

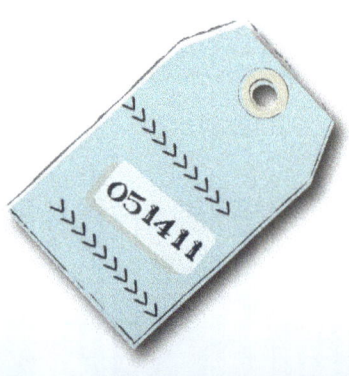

Notes

Let's Stay Informed

This book includes a wealth of valuable resources, websites, programs, and references carefully gathered to support you. As information continues to evolve, you can revisit these resources for the most up-to-date insights.

"Seeking wisdom and being informed are cornerstones of growth, empowering you to make thoughtful decisions and confidently navigate life's ever-changing landscape."
— Kathleen Cesarin, LPN

Recommended Resources

TOPIC	WEBSITE / RESOURCES
Meals, Physical Health, and Safety	**Alberta Elder Abuse - Staying Safe: A Resource for Older Adults** *(https://albertaelderabuse.ca/resources/ staying-safe-a-resource-for-older-adults-living-in-alberta)* **Canadian Dental Care Plan (CDCP)** *(http://www.canada.ca/dental)* **Finding Balance Alberta - Are You at Risk of Falling Assessment** *(https://www.findingbalancealberta.ca/)* **Grocery Delivery - Instacart** *(https://www.instacart.ca/)* **Grocery Delivery - PC Express** *(https://www.pcexpress.ca/)* **Grocery Delivery - Walmart** *(https://www.walmart.ca/en/dp/ landing-page?icid=cp_l1_page_grocery_delivery_pass_42528_T8KZHPYEJB)* **Heart to Home Meals - Canada/USA** *(https://www.hearttohomemeals.ca/)* **Home Care - Home Instead** *(https://www.homeinstead.ca/ppc/home-care/)* **Home Care - Nurse Next Door** *(https://www.nursenextdoor.com/)* **Home Care - Qualicare** *(https://qualicare.com/)* **Home & Community Care - AHS - Canada** *(https://www.albertahealthservices.ca/ cc/page15488.aspx)* **Meals on Wheels - Canada** *(https://healthyagingcore.ca/ featured-programs-and-initiatives/meals-on-wheels)* **Meals on Wheels - USA** *(https://www.mealsonwheelsamerica.org/)* **What to Do When Someone Else Dies - Canada** *(https://www.canada.ca/en/ services/life-events/death.html)*

TOPIC	WEBSITE / RESOURCES
Housing	**A Place for Mom** (https://www.aplaceformom.com/) **Canada Mortgage and Housing Corporation (CMHC)** (https://www.cmhc-schl.gc.ca/) **CARP (Canadian Association of Retired Persons)** (https://www.carp.ca/) **Chartwell Retirement Residences** (https://chartwell.com/) **Comfort Life** (https://www.comfortlife.ca/) **Greater Edmonton Foundation - Affordable/Subsidized** (https://gef.org/) **Heartland Housing - Affordable/Subsidized** (https://www.heartlandhousing.ca/) **Homeland Housing - Affordable/Subsidized** (https://homelandhousing.ca/) **Leading Age** (https://www.leadingage.org/) **National Institute on Aging** (https://www.nia.nih.gov/) **RetirementHomes.com** (https://www.retirementhomes.com/) **SeniorHousingNet.com** (https://www.seniorhousingnet.com/) **SeniorLiving.org** (https://www.seniorliving.org/) **Senior Housing Programs in Canada** (https://www.canada.ca/en/financial-consumer-agency/services/retirement-planning/cost-seniors-housing.html#toc2)
Government Programs	**Family and Community Support Services (FCSS) of Alberta** (https://www.alberta.ca/family-and-community-support-services-fcss-program) **Government of Canada - Seniors Programs & Services** (https://www.canada.ca/en/employment-social-development/campaigns/seniors.html) **Medicaid Cash and Counseling Programs - Self Directed Services - USA** (https://www.medicaid.gov/medicaid/long-term-services-supports/self-directed-services/index.html) **Medicare - USA** (https://www.medicare.gov/) **National Family Caregiver Support Program - USA** (https://acl.gov/programs/support-caregivers/national-family-caregiver-support-program) **Program of All-Inclusive Care for the Elderly - PACE -USA** (https://www.cms.gov/medicare/medicaid-coordination/about/pace) **Prosper Canada Benefits Wayfinder** (https://prospercanada.org/) **Retirement Planning & Living (CPP/OAS/GIS/Disability) - CANADA** (https://www.canada.ca/en/employment-social-development/campaigns/retirement-planning.html?utm_campaign=esdc-edsc-services_for_seniors-24-25&utm_source=ggl&utm_medium=sem&utm_content=ad-text_en&adv=2425-670505&utm_term=apply+for+canada+pension+plan&gad_source=1&gclid=EAIaIQobChMIvJ_zml-DjAMVowetBh2-oQA2EAAYASAAEgKV6vD_BwE&gclsrc=aw.ds) **USA Government - Benefit Finder - Retirement** (https://www.usa.gov/benefit-finder/retirement) **Veterans Affairs Canada** (https://www.veterans.gc.ca/en) **Veterans Affairs USA** (https://www.va.gov/)

TOPIC	WEBSITE / RESOURCES
General / International Older Adult Advocacy	**AARP International** (https://www.aarpinternational.org/) **AGE of Central Texas** (https://ageofcentraltx.org/) **Age International** (https://www.ageinternational.org.uk/) **Age Platform Europe** (https://www.age-platform.eu/) **American Society on Aging** (https://www.asaging.org/) **Balancing Work & Caregiving Responsibilities** (https://www.canada.ca/en/employment-social-development/corporate/seniors-forum-federal-provincial-territorial/tips-caregivers.html) **Canadian Home Care Association** (https://cdnhomecare.ca/campaign-better-home-care-in-canada-a-national-action-plan/) **Caregivers Alberta** (http://www.caregiversalberta.ca/) **Global Alliance for the Rights of Older People (GAROP)** (https://rightsofolderpeople.org/) **Government of Canada Benefits Finder** (https://srv138.services.gc.ca/daf/q?id=0183c096-f093-47ee-9719-033b37ed9195&goctemplateculture=en-ca) **Healthy Aging CORE (Collaborative Online Resources and Education)** https://healthyagingcore.ca/ **Help Age Canada** (https://www.helpagecanada.ca/) **Help Age International** (https://www.helpage.org/) **International Association of Gerontology and Geriatrics (IAGG)** (https://www.iagg.info/) **International Federation on Ageing (IFA)** (https://ifa.ngo/) **International Longevity Centre Global Alliance (ILC-GA)** (https://www.ilc-alliance.org/) **International Men's Shed Organisation** (https://menshed.com/) **Sage Seniors Association** (http://www.mysage.ca/)
Innovative Examples of Older Adult Living from Around the World	**Abbeyfield Houses - Canada** (https://abbeyfield.ca/) **Dementia Village - Netherlands** (https://hogeweyk.dementiavillage.com/) **Homes For Heroes - Canada** (https://homesforheroesfoundation.ca/) **Home Share Pilot - Canada** (https://homeshareto.ca/) **Indigenous Elders Lodge** (https://www.cmhc-schl.gc.ca/media-newsroom/news-releases/2024/affordable-homes-indigenous-elders-municipal-district-greenview) **Innovative Architectural Design - Australia** (https://architectus.com.au/latest/the-future-of-senior-living-design-to-empower-older-australians/) **Mixed Use Developments - USA** (https://www.aegisliving.com/locations/aegis-gardens-newcastle-wa/) **Multigenerational Program - Finland** (https://www.agedcareguide.com.au/talking-aged-care/youths-living-with-the-elderly-a-finnish-example) **Nordic Independent Living Challenge** (https://www.nordicinnovation.org/realchallenge) **Retiring on a Cruise Ship** (https://pmc.ncbi.nlm.nih.gov/articles/PMC526150/) **Village to Village Network** (https://www.vtvnetwork.org/content.aspx?page_id=0&club_id=691012) **Wisdom in Design - Jim Gladue - Indigenous Architect** (http://gladuedesigns.wixsite.com/gladuedesigns)

TOPIC	WEBSITE / RESOURCES
Emotional / Spiritual / Holistic Wellness	**Dr. Joe Dispenza - Rewired Series** (*https://gaia.everflowclient.io/affiliate/signup/?p=88WP91S1*) **International Men's Shed Organisation** (*https://menshed.com/*) **My Inner Strength Knows No Bounds** (*https://www.amazon.ca/My-Inner-Strength-Knows-Bounds/dp/B09ZL9BQW8/*) **Pearl Gregor, PhD, Author, and Dream Coach** (*http://www.dreamsalongtheway.com/*) **The Law Depot** (*https://www.lawdepot.ca/*)
Financial / Retirement Planning	**Canadian Retirement Income Calculator** (*https://www.canada.ca/en/services/benefits/publicpensions/cpp/retirement-income-calculator.html*) **Primerica - Derrick Cunningham** (*https://www.primerica.com/cunninghams*) **Retirement Readiness Quiz - Canada** (*https://www.canada.ca/en/services/retirement/quiz-main.html*) **What to Do When Someone Else Dies - Canada** (*https://www.canada.ca/en/services/life-events/death.html*)

Bibliography

Books

Cameron, Julia. It's Never Too Late to Begin Again: Discovering Creativity and Meaning at Midlife and Beyond. New York: TarcherPerigee, 2016.

Dispenza, Joe. Becoming Supernatural: How Common People Are Doing the Uncommon. Carlsbad, CA: Hay House, 2017.

Breaking the Habit of Being Yourself: How to Lose Your Mind and Create a New One. Carlsbad, CA: Hay House, 2012. Green, Lyndsay. You Could Live a Long Time: Are You Ready? Toronto: HarperCollins Canada, 2010.

Kortes-Miller, Kathy. Talking About Death Won't Kill You: The Essential Guide to End-of-Life Conversations. Toronto: ECW Press, 2018.

Levy, Becca. Breaking the Age Code: How Your Beliefs About Aging Determine How Long and Well You Live. New York: William Morrow, 2022.

Walker, Matthew. Why We Sleep: Unlocking the Power of Sleep and Dreams. New York: Scribner, 2017.

Web Resources

Age International. "Support for Older People Worldwide." Accessed July 14, 2025. https://www.ageinternational.org.uk/

Alberta Elder Abuse Awareness Council. "Staying Safe: A Resource for Older Adults Living in Alberta." Accessed July 14, 2025. https://albertaelderabuse.ca/resources/staying-safe-a-resource-for-older-adults-living-in-alberta

Alberta Health Services. "Continuing Care Services." Accessed July 14, 2025. https://www.albertahealthservices.ca/cc/page15488.aspx American Society on Aging. "Aging Resources and Advocacy." Accessed July 14, 2025. https://www.asaging.org/

Canada.ca. "Your Aging Checklist: A Seniors' Self-Assessment Tool." Employment and Social Development Canada. Accessed July 14, 2025. https://www.canada.ca/content/dam/canada/employment-social-development/corporate/seniors/forum/aging-checklist/aging-checklist- seniors-EN.pdf

Canada Mortgage and Housing Corporation. "Affordable Homes for Indigenous Elders in the Municipal District of Greenview." Published 2024. https://www.cmhc-schl.gc.ca/media-newsroom/news-releases/2024/affordable-homes-indigenous-elders-municipal-district-greenview

Centers for Medicare & Medicaid Services. "Programs of All-Inclusive Care for the Elderly (PACE)." Accessed July 14, 2025. https://www.cms.gov/medicare/medicaid-coordination/about/pace

Global Alliance for the Rights of Older People. "Advocacy for Older Adults' Rights." Accessed July 14, 2025. https://rightsofolderpeople.org/

Government of Canada. "Direct Assessment Form for Seniors' Benefits." Accessed July 14, 2025. https://srv138.services.gc.ca/daf/q? id=0183c096-f093-47ee-9719-033b37ed9195&goctemplateculture=en-ca

"Support for Seniors." Accessed July 14, 2025. https://www.canada.ca/en/employment-social-development/campaigns/seniors.html

HelpAge Canada. "Supporting Seniors in Canada." Accessed July 14, 2025. https://helpagecanada.ca/ HelpAge International. "Global Aging Support." Accessed July 14, 2025. https://www.helpage.org/

International Federation on Ageing. "Global Aging Advocacy and Research." Accessed July 14, 2025. https://ifa.ngo/ LawDepot. "Legal Document Services." Accessed July 14, 2025. https://www.lawdepot.ca/

Men's Shed Canada. "Men's Shed Canada." Accessed July 14, 2025. https://menshed.com/

National Institute on Aging. "Research and Resources on Aging." Accessed July 14, 2025. https://www.nia.nih.gov/

Nordic Innovation. "Real Challenge Initiative." Accessed July 14, 2025. https://www.nordicinnovation.org/realchallenge

Sage Seniors Association. "Supporting Seniors in Alberta." Accessed July 14, 2025. https://www.mysage.ca/ USA.gov.

"Retirement Benefit Finder." Accessed July 14, 2025. https://www.usa.gov/benefit-finder/retirement Medicare.gov.

"Official U.S. Government Site for Medicare." Accessed July 14, 2025. https://www.medicare.gov/

Academic Articles and Media

Dispenza, Joe. Rewired with Dr. Joe Dispenza. Gaia, 2019.

Hirshkowitz, Max, et al. "National Sleep Foundation's Sleep Time Duration Recommendations: Methodology and Results Summary." Sleep Health 1, no. 1 (2015): 40–43.

Irwin, Michael R. "Why Sleep Is Important for Health: A Psychoneuroimmunology Perspective." Psychoneuroendocrinology 57 (2015): 163–78.

Xie, Lulu, et al. "Sleep Drives Metabolite Clearance from the Adult Brain." Science 342, no. 6156 (2013): 373–77. https://doi.org/10.1126/science.1241224

Acknowledgement

Creating **Living & Aging Well** has been a journey fueled by collaboration, innovation, and a shared vision of a more inclusive, holistic, and empowered approach to aging. This book is more than a resource—it is a movement toward progressive, transparent, and inclusive discussions on how we support older adults, caregivers, families, and professionals in navigating life's transitions with dignity and confidence.

It is with deep gratitude that I recognize:

Dr. Pearl Gregor, PhD
Author and Owner of Dreams Along The Way

for her generous support and commitment to making this guide possible.

Please visit her at www.dreamsalongtheway.com to learn more about her, her dream work and her transformational books.

Join in Shaping the Future of Living and Aging Well

The conversation doesn't stop here.

Aging is a lifelong journey, and we invite more changemakers, thought leaders, and organizations to be part of this growing movement.

- ✓ Would you like to support a future edition?
- ✓ Interested in co-branding, customized editions, or speaking engagements?
- ✓ Do you have an inspiring initiative that aligns with my mission?
- ✓ Are you interested in bulk discounts and the permission to resell the book to support your organization or event?

I'd love to hear from you! Let's continue building a future where holistic living and aging is embraced, supported, and celebrated.

Get in touch: kathleen@philosophiawithin.com Learn more: www.philosophiawithin.com

With gratitude,

Kathleen Cesarin, LPN
Author, *Living and Aging Well*

www.ingramcontent.com/pod-product-compliance
Lightning Source LLC
Chambersburg PA
CBHW041512120626

46551CB00018B/2400